The Service Journey

Developing and implementing a service strategy that works for you, your business, department, or organization

Susan J. Hoekstra

Aventine Press

Published by Aventine Press
750 State St. #319
San Diego CA, 92101

ISBN: 1-59330-587-7
Printed in the United States of America.

I dedicate this book to my parents, Jim and Margaret,
who taught me right from wrong,

to my sons Ben and Matt who inspire me to be my best,

and to everyone who provides life's most difficult
experiences, who make me determined
to overcome.

Table of Contents

Forward

There are lots of books on the market regarding service. Let's face it; everyone who shops or frequents restaurants believes they are experts in the topic. We all know when we have had a good experience and remember far longer those poor service experiences. I too have admittedly received some of my expertise from the front-line, having braved the stores and the lines; the good and the bad.

I have gained knowledge from the statistics and the work of researchers who have proven that great service over time leads to greater profitability. Most notably, I have fervently read and listened to the likes of Fred Reichheld, author of *Loyalty Rules*, Jill Griffin, author of *Customer Loyalty: How to Earn It, How to Keep It,* and Dennis Snow, author of *Lessons from the Mouse.* I have also analyzed the models of firms known for service, such as The Ritz-Carlton, Disney, and Nordstrom.

I have gained conviction of these truths from the experiences of my life. For I am the person who worked for five companies that all ultimately went out of business or went through major restructuring. Not that any of these issues were my fault; I did my work well. And, especially after the first time a company I worked for imploded, I made sure I reviewed their balance sheets and profitability very carefully before agreeing to work at any of those businesses. *I* interviewed *them* and made sure I looked for firms that were stable and had been in business for many decades. However, after joining each firm, invariably each company closed or completely reorganized either through a sale, discontinuation of their US distribution, unsuccessful leveraged buyout, unprecedented fraud, or market collapse. Each of these experiences honed my core belief that formulated my service conviction, which can be summarized in one statement; behavior ultimately results in consequences – good or bad.

I also gained my service expertise in spite of the fact that my early career and educational concentration was spent in very traditional accounting and finance roles. I earned two bachelors degrees; having returned to school for my second degree after finding out no one was impressed with my ever vague Bachelors Degree with a business and economics major. After earning this first degree, I found I was only able to find a job as a teller at a bank, hence the second degree. My second Bachelor's Degree was earned part time at night and I literally chose my major by looking in the classified section of the newspaper to see what jobs were available. I didn't look far as I ended up majoring in accounting. I used education once again as my catalyst to escape my environment while I worked with the company ultimately found with fraud; that time I earned my MBA in Finance.

The firm where the fraud was found marked a major change in my career. Before that, people I worked with strictly knew me as an accounting or finance expert, albeit an atypical finance professional. For example, in the firm that ultimately discontinued their US distributions, I started in accounts receivable and took over general ledger and financial statement responsibilities. Management loved me because I literally replaced three people who had worked at the firm before. Employees hated me for the same reason; I literally replaced three of their friends with whom they had worked for as many as twenty years. Even when I left three years later, I was still the new person at the firm. I did have front to back P&L and Balance Sheet experience; however, something that would have taken me many more years to attain if I had worked in a more stable environment.

I received a job offer from a jukebox and vending machine manufacturing firm that was in business for 40 – 50 years. A good stable business; I had finally made it. Within a year of my arrival, however, the company went through an unsuccessful leveraged buyout. I was initially hired to analyze accounts; because of the leveraged buyout, I became responsible for the forecast and cash management as well. I had to prepare for weekly meetings with bankers to explain how we were going to meet our debt obligation and had meetings with senior managers who had been in business for years, telling them they were going to go out of business if they continued to conduct business in the same fashion as they were. After I delivered this last bit of bad news, the senior management hired a consultant to review my analysis and to explain to me where I had gone wrong. After all, I was only 27 years old at the time; there was no way I could have foreseen the imminent collapse of a major company. After reviewing my work, the consultant asked if I had showed management my analysis.

9

"Yes", I replied.

"And what did they say?"

"They called you to show me why I was wrong."

He paused, smiled ruefully and told me I probably learned more in my very short career than many learn in decades. While I appreciated all this knowledge, all this real life education was painful. A few months earlier, the CFO, who I had a great relationship with, had left the company (something I've learned is never a good sign) and I now reported to the Cost Accountant turned acting CFO, who, in my opinion, knew very little about cash management and leveraged buyouts.

The epitome of my experience working for Mr. Cost Accountant was the day I quit. I had worked until 11pm the night before, putting together an analysis for him to use with the bankers; working very late and coming in very early were commonplace. I had prepared the document on an excel spreadsheet. "Why didn't you put this on a 3 x 5 card for me? I can't believe you didn't put this on a 3 x 5 card!" he snarled. Who would put an analysis on a 3 x 5 card unless they were explicitly asked to? I had never put any of our analysis on 3 x 5 cards before. Even so, if his tone was even remotely human, I would happily oblige. Being screamed at first thing in the morning after working so many hours was more than I could take; I reached my breaking point. I interviewed with thirty different companies at this point and was extremely stressed out with the weekly bank meetings. I therefore did what everyone probably dreams of doing, at least once in their life: I took the analysis, ripped it into hundreds of pieces, and threw the paper in the air like confetti. I think I surprised myself as much as I surprised him. I left his office shaking with anger and went outside to the parking lot to calm down. Of course, had I pre-planned this, I would have had my purse with my license and keys with me so I could go home, but I hadn't and so I couldn't. I walked around for twenty minutes before returning to my desk. He was waiting for me and asked me if I didn't feel better. I presumed he was joking, so I didn't respond. When I looked at my desk, I saw the job offer had come in from the company that I interviewed with, that I was most interested. It was in Stamford Connecticut and I lived in New Jersey, a one hundred mile commute round-trip, but that didn't matter at this point. It was an interesting job, I was desperate; I could handle it. I called them, had them fax over the offer and gave my notice that day.

At that moment something else happened. I became personally convicted that my spiritual faith was real; I knew I was being taken care of. How could the timing of that job offer been any better? Yes, I was interviewing, but as anyone who interviews knows, just because you interview doesn't mean you find a great position. The economy at the time wasn't good and besides, I was picky. I already had a bad job and I didn't want to switch just to change jobs. I wanted a better opportunity at a better firm. Divine intervention stepped in that day to save me from that situation.

Within a year, Mr. Cost Accountant and a few other employees who had worked with the firm for years moved to Texas because the company merged with another. I do not believe the newly formed company was viable and often wondered what happened to the people with whom I worked. I once drove by the old manufacturing site where

I worked. What was once vibrant was now vacant, a sea of overgrown grass, and broken glass.

I moved on to a new adventure, however. I had finally made it. I joined a membership services company. The first few years were fine. I was responsible for the payroll, cash management, stock purchase plan and stock option plans. I automated all of the areas I was responsible and was promoted to Director. I thought I had finally found a company that was successful. What I didn't know was that I worked with employees who would ultimately plead guilty for committing fraud seven years later. The signs were there. First the CFO quit (again, never a good sign). My boss became the CFO and I started reporting to a different person. Although I was never asked to do anything illegal, it was during this time that I was asked to do unethical things, creating a very uncomfortable work environment. I have always been the person who was the star employee. I work hard, achieve more than identified objectives and develop creative solutions that automate processes. I also improve the experience and save money. With each firm or department that I have worked, I have always been replaced by multiple people after I have submitted my resignation.

The catalyst came when, after four years with the company, my new boss asked that I send employee records to an insurance sales company so they could develop individual benefits statements for employees and set up mandatory one-on-one meetings with the employees, showing them the value of their benefits and their need for supplemental life insurance. In other words, these employees who trusted us, who were barely making more than minimum wage and who needed to support their families, were going to be subjected to mandatory high-pressure sales from an insurance salesperson who knew everything about the person including how many dependents the individual had. Since I was responsible for payroll, I was asked to send the information. I refused.

I still remember my boss asking me why I couldn't simply acknowledge that it was wrong, but to do it because my company had asked me to. That logic didn't work for me, however. Wrong was wrong and at the end of the day I needed to live with myself. A few years later she was testifying in court regarding her involvement with the financial statement fraud.

I'd love to tell you that things took care of themselves when I said I wouldn't cooperate, but they didn't, and I almost lost my job. I had to go to the human resources department, because technically I was being defiant and refusing to follow orders. It was again a very low time in my life. The company never did send the records to the insurance company and did ultimately sever the relationship, but it was a very uncomfortable working situation after that nonetheless.

I requested a move into another department just to buy time. You see, I still had a year left before I would earn my MBA and I didn't want to leave until I could add that MBA credential to my resume. I was offered a job as the Director of Customer Service, working with corporate clients. It was a newly created department, and I was the manager. We provided analysis for corporate clients that forecast how much money they could make if they marketed with us. We also explained their actual results and analyzed variances, went on sales calls, and presented at client meetings. Near the end of the year with my newly formed group, while I was finishing my MBA, I planned to begin looking for another job once again. However, just as I was beginning my job search, my firm merged with another company much closer to my home; again, divine intervention. Who could have scripted a better outcome to my long tortuous ordeal? I was able to transfer to the new headquarters office close to my home as the Director and later VP of Budgets Analysis and Efficiencies for their 42 contact centers (contact centers are those places that accept your hotel or car rental reservations). I had finally made it.

I was able to use all of my analytical knowledge to help make good business decisions, and apply the lessons learned from the decisions that hurt my prior firms as well. I realized that it was important to maintain a balance between costs, employee satisfaction and service to the clients. If all we focused on was efficiency, we were able to reduce the cost-per-call, in the short term; however, our sales and employee satisfaction suffered. It required a balance of all three: expense control and employee and client satisfaction, so that great service (and ultimately optimized profits) was realized. I had learned first hand the negative impact of what happened when people forgot the human element of the job and only focused on short term objectives. Ultimately the numbers suffered as well. So I ensured all our analysis would encourage managers to maintain a balance between the three.

I really enjoyed this job. It enabled me to travel across the country and even the world to meet people with different perspectives and cultures, giving me an appreciation for the various viewpoints of people. That job only lasted a few years, however. Fraud was found soon after the merger, at the firm I had left behind in Connecticut. The people I worked with, who were involved with the fraud lost everything, had their names in the paper and ended up with probation, narrowly escaping jail sentences. The top two executives of the firm, however, weren't so lucky and were sent to prison for multiyear sentences. The company never did really succeed after that, and the entire firm, including my new area, was eventually divested. Employee and shareholder wealth was once again decimated.

I was gone before the divestiture actually happened. I took a package and moved on with a colleague in hopes of opening my own consulting company. Let's face it, many of us have dreamed of having no boss and I was no different. In fact, my work experience probably gave me even more incentive than most not to stay in the corporate world. Besides, working with the contact centers and seeing what happens when managers make extreme decisions that benefit only the company's profits at the expense of employees and/or clients made me want to use that experience and expertise to help other companies avoid some of the same mistakes.

I liked working with different companies as well. Typically, what I found is that the owner or manager had one viewpoint, but the employees would then tell you what actually happened. I also learned from companies who did things well; that didn't look to cut corners and who took care of their clients and their employees, ultimately taking care of their shareholders and investors.

What I hadn't considered is how hard it is to start your own business, and how there is absolutely no support to help you get things done. My children, who were only four and six at the time, were literally drafted to help me stuff envelopes and put together mailings. In addition, instead of having no boss, I now had many bosses, and, because you are working for more than one person, you are also either really busy, or not busy at all. That would be fine if the money came in steadily, but I soon discovered it didn't. Unfortunately, I couldn't get my bills to come at the same rate as the money, so I started looking for a corporate job six months after opening my new consulting company, two weeks before Christmas. I was offered three jobs within weeks and accepted a position as the VP of Service Strategy and Collaboration of a large multi-billion dollar corporation six months before September 11. Now I had finally made it!

I have spent eight years in my current position; the cultural change experts will tell you it takes approximately eight years to see change. The change has been slow-going, has been inconsistent and has sometimes been painful. It requires a lot of work and the perseverance of many. But the change has also been real. I see it and hear it in the stories, in employee's behavior, and in the satisfaction of the clients.

This book represents what I've learned through all of this experience, so you can embark on your own journey and learn from my mistakes. Whether you are a manager at a large or small company, or are an independent contributor, this book will reflect a compilation of all my experience that can help you implement a personalized service culture where you work.

You will also find the book is intentionally vague at times, for two reasons. First, your service delivery is going to be unique from that of another firm, store, office or department; what works for you may not work for them.

You will need to customize the recommendations for your situation, your culture, your environment. However, the book's service-experience examples are also intentionally vague at times, because the concepts apply for all businesses, and although there are differences between businesses, there are also similarities that transcend industries and situations.

This book will demonstrate how doing what is right by the client, how a lot of hard work and how persistence for doing what is important is going to ultimately result in change that ultimately impacts the bottom line.

"We are what we repeatedly do.
Excellence, then, is not an act, but a habit."

\- Aristotle

Step 1: Beginning the Journey

If you are reading this book, you may want to implement a formal service strategy, or more likely, improve the service delivery of your department, business, firm, or store. Or, you may in fact be struggling, wondering why all of your efforts haven't paid off already, and wondering if you're focusing on the right things, on what is really important. You want that competitive advantage over your competition and want to know how you can achieve that most easily. Your firm, store, or department may currently be large or small; unprofitable or profitable.

In many ways, being established and profitable makes it more difficult to implement a service strategy. This is true because employees of profitable firms are more likely to be set in their ways. Their behavior has worked for them in the past and they have been successful, possibly both personally and on a company-wide level for many years. Many employees also work their entire careers at one firm, and therefore only have that one company from which they draw their experience. They are making money; there is no pressing reason they really need to change. In some cases, the culture may even encourage employees to be non-service oriented.

For example, in some of the firms I have worked, many decisions were made based upon whether those decisions would help the firm hit the current quarter's forecast. Headcount may have been added and/or taken away and projects started and ended based upon whether that quarter's goals were going to be met.

Service is a long-term commitment however. When you implement a service strategy, make no mistake about it. You are changing the culture of the company. Who is hired, what is rewarded, and how decisions are made are all critical. Service impacts the products and processes, and service also changes conversations, the viewpoint and the vision of employees. What was considered acceptable behavior before may not be considered acceptable in the service-oriented culture.

Indeed, you or your employees may even be afraid that by being client-focused, the firm will become unprofitable. I frequently hear comments similar to this "We can make our customers happy if we give away everything for free, but then we won't be able to make any money," as if you can't have good service without foregoing profitability. Obviously, going out of business is not the goal, and comparable to companies that cut costs in order to hit current quarters' forecast, companies that employ too many people, take on too much debt, or sell product at the wrong price are also implementing short-term strategies that cannot be sustained in the long term.

The fact is, studies show that firms who are known for service are actually more profitable than their competitors, and can charge more for their services. Companies may be able to get by with non-service-oriented strategies in the short-term, but in the long-term a company can have a competitive advantage if they adapt a comprehensive service strategy. In Frederick Reichheld's book The *Loyalty Effect*, Reichheld demonstrates the superior customer value that is achieved when investor or shareholder, employee, and customer loyalty are all achieved.

Since you are reading this book, you probably also believe giving good service is important, and may even talk about service with conviction at times. Every one of us recognizes when we've personally received a good or poor service experience and we are quick to criticize the service delivery of others. Employees usually believe they also personally deliver great service; although they frequently acknowledge the people they work with aren't good service providers at all. If the beliefs of the individual service provider were all true, however, and each one of us was delivering such great service, we'd all be having much better experiences.

When implementing a service culture, even if everyone initially seems to embrace the concept, there invariably will come a point you lose people. That is when people realize good service requires them personally to change their behavior, regardless of who they are in the organization. A service commitment impacts personal behavior, not some of the time, but constantly, and it is hard work. I like to compare it to going on a diet. You can agree with the concept, read books, and speak about it with conviction, but unless you change your eating and exercise habits and do so consistently, you will not realize an impact. The same is true for delivering excellent service; good service requires hard work and commitment.

If you look at the definition for service in Webster's Dictionary, it will say service is to "aid, assist, help." The very nature of the definition implies that we are aiding, assisting and helping the customer or client. However, service also insinuates and necessitates a much broader definition and scope than one that impacts only front-line employees. Ultimately, being service-oriented will impact everything: your location, building, and layout of your store; it will impact your products, website, the people you hire, the back-end process, sales, and marketing. Service will impact everything, because everything in your organization exists ultimately for the client. In a society that is looking for short-term profits, this may be a foreign concept and may be why most organizations fall short of the goal. Service is all-encompassing, and it is all about the client. Therefore, in order to really have a good service environment, you need to make all decisions, have all conversations, and develop technology, programs or products consistently with your clients' best interest at heart. *Service is branding your clients' experience.*

Let me illustrate why it's necessary to make your definition of service so comprehensive. I have purchased two identical cars, within nine years, from the same dealer. I was able to drive my first car for 170,000 miles before it finally had a heart attack and died (a death is the only way to describe it as literally the transmission, radiator and engine all went at the same time). Although I've always really liked the car, I must admit I have an issue with the service department. It's not that they're not nice; they're actually very service-oriented when you evaluate them from a limited service perspective. However, every time I go there I feel as if they're ripping me off. For example, they once told me there were a few minor things wrong with my car and gave me a price of $2500 to have it repaired.

The price was literally three times more than I ultimately paid by bringing my car elsewhere. After this incident, I avoided the dealer's service department whenever I could, but once had no choice but to take it back when my auto body shop diagnosed an issue that only the dealer could fix, so I reluctantly took it back. Although I told the service department what was wrong with the car, they charged me an hours' worth of fees to diagnose the same issue. $120 and they hadn't even started working! A third time I had a mirror that became cloudy over time. Personally, I would have ignored it, but my car failed inspection, so I went to the parts department for a new mirror. Because the mirror was attached to a mechanical mounting that you could adjust from inside the car, I figured it would be pretty involved to replace it, and I wasn't sure anyone but the dealer would be familiar with the mechanics. So I reluctantly asked service how much it would cost. I was told $120. At this point, I figured I had nothing to lose, pried off the old mirror with a coin, and snapped the new one in place within seconds. It worked perfectly.

The point is this. With each encounter, the employees themselves were very nice. That wasn't enough to make me feel as if I received good service, though, because I repeatedly felt as if they tried to take advantage of me. Although I love the car, as soon as the warranty is off, I immediately go to my local mechanic for service, because I trust him to fix my car at a fair price.

This story illustrates the fact that the issues your clients may have with your service may not have anything to do with what you traditionally consider to be service. If all you address with your service strategy is whether or not your employees are professional, you undoubtedly will still have very unhappy clients. Therefore, expand your definition of service and realize that everything that touches your client ultimately weighs in on their evaluation as to whether or not they've had a good experience, and whether or not they want to continue doing business with you.

Ideally, in order to truly succeed, a service culture needs to be implemented from the top down; from the most senior executives down to the front-line employees within the organization, everyone needs to be aligned. If you are not in a position to make this commitment for your firm, you still can have limited success on a regional-, office-, or even a department-level. Regardless of whether you are implementing a service strategy for a large or small firm, department or store, begin by developing something simple, visionary and something senior executives can speak to easily. Although details are necessary for line managers and front-line employees, initially produce something high level that is flexible enough to be appropriate for everyone. Ideally the communications should also be inspirational and aspirational.

For small organizations, start developing your service strategy by creating a service team with representation from the impacted areas. This will allow for cross-functional representation and buy-in. Team members should be leaders within the organization, will help implement the team's decisions, and be held accountable to the team.

Similarly, for firm-wide initiatives, start developing your service strategy by creating a centralized service department whose purpose is to advocate on behalf of the client and align the organization and firm's employees. Organize your new department so it is neutral, not located within any business area, with service authority over all business areas within the firm.

Furthermore, review your firm's entire organizational structure and identify areas within the firm that directly impact the client, such as your phone centers, the website, statements, segmentation, billing, or pricing. For all client-facing areas, create a dual-reporting role for the managers of these areas, so that they report both into their functional area and into the newly created centralized service organization. This will help align the entire organization, and circumvent the silos that tend to create inconsistent client experiences. To the client, of course, there is no differentiation between the product and the sale, pricing, website, customer service, or the front-line employee; they all provide one comprehensive branded experience. To the organization, each experience is determined independently and provided by a different department. As such, it is necessary for the company to review itself as their clients view them; a matrixed organization helps support that.

Let's review this recommendation to see how it would work in practice, and let's take phone centers, or contact centers as our example. Let's assume our fictitious organization produces widgets; in order to keep it simple we have only one client, and to support this one client we have set up three phone centers: one to generate the sale, one for customer support and one phone center to answer billing questions and to collect our money. The employees who work in our phone centers report into various areas within the firm: Sales, Operations, and Finance. However, if the three managers who run our contact centers don't have a dual reporting line, our one and only client will have an extremely different experience depending upon where they call. Phones within the three departments will be set up differently, departments staffed differently, and inconsistent professional skills training completed. Our client may even receive three phone numbers to reach the three departments; come into contact with phone prompts with the first number, a long wait for the second number, and a voice-mail box attached to the third.

If, on the other hand, the managers of all three departments have a dual reporting structure, reporting not only into their traditional reporting line, but also into this centralized service organization, our client's experience will at minimum be consistent (we will work on making it great later). Left to their own devices, the managers of the various departments are going to evaluate good service differently, have conflicting objectives, and be less likely to take a holistic approach to our client's experience. Some managers will want to set the objectives for answering the phones faster, some slower. Some managers won't consider it important to train phone staff on professional skills while others will. Some departments will be more staffed than others; some could even be over-staffed, while other areas are understaffed. If you are truly going to make an impact on the service delivered and provide a consistently excellent experience, you need to centrally manage your clients' experience. A dual reporting role for client-facing areas will help facilitate this, integrating impacted employees both into the business area they support, as well as the service organization. By implementing this dual reporting structure, you can leverage training, technology, facilities, staffing, and budgets and analysis consistently across all areas impacted.

The accounting for our matrixed organization holds the centralized service department responsible for managing the fixed costs in total and variable costs on a per unit basis. In our phone center example, our variable costs are direct labor plus telecom and we divide the variable costs by call volume in order to calculate the per unit cost. The matrixed organization holds the departments being supported responsible for forecasting the volume of business, and those departments receive a chargeback of the budgeted variable costs per unit on an actual volume basis.

So, going back to our example with the phone centers, let's assume our centralized service department tells our support departments they can answer calls at a variable cost of $3 per call, based upon an assumption of 1,000 calls, a number provided by the support department. Let's further assume our support department manufactures a new product or service with a lot of defects, and decides to launch it anyway. Call volume therefore increases to 1,500 calls, not the 1,000 originally forecast. Service is still responsible for answering calls at $3 per call, however, they charge our support department $4,500 (1,500 * $3) instead of the $3000 our support department originally expected; they are therefore held accountable and incented to deliver new services or products that are error-free, intuitive, and a benefit to the client. In this same example, as call volume increases, service levels at the contact center are kept steady because the centralized service department is empowered to move employees around and hire additional staff if necessary. This structure aligns the two areas of the organization for the benefit of the client, to ensure a consistent service experience, and to hold both areas accountable for what they control.

Other areas that perform similar functions, impact the client and reside in multiple organizational units within the firm should also be reviewed to determine if they could benefit from dual-reporting lines. For example, written client communications may consist of the website, statements, brochures, marketing material, and other miscellaneous information. If it is not centrally managed, communications may not be coordinated, there may not be a similar look and feel to the work produced, there may even be conflicting information sent to clients. By branding the clients' experience via our centralized service department, and creating dual reporting roles you are able to take a holistic approach to your clients' experience.

Once your client-focused corporate structure is in place, we can then create a service mission or vision statement; a corporate philosophy that guides employees' behavior when situations come up that aren't defined or expected. For as detailed as you may be with your service standards, there will be things and issues that come up that you will not envision; undefined situations that may create a great source of service dissatisfaction for your clients. Undefined situations are to be expected, as you don't want to risk the chance your employees behave like robots, and you won't be able to make every decision, or influence every conversation yourself. To avoid client dissatisfaction and provide a great experience, the mission or vision statement provides your employees with confidence and the flexibility to make decisions, because they understand the ultimate objective.

For firms known for great service, having a service mission or vision statement is commonplace. For example, at the Ritz Carlton, it is every employee's responsibility to make partners and customers satisfied. At Disney, every employee has the responsibility to create happiness. At TD Bank, their mission is to be convenient.

The mission or vision statement at these firms is then translated by every single employee within the company into something concrete that is used to guide behavior. And, although there is extensive training at these firms, employees know what to do even when they encounter something that hasn't been defined. For a client, the service mission statement translates into a great service experience.

This is why a guest at Disney, will most likely receive a replacement popcorn if they accidentally drop theirs. If the Disney employee sees it, they have a mission to create happiness. Have you ever thought of what you would do if you went to a Disney park and forgot where you parked? There are thousands of cars that park in the lot on any given day and to make matters worse, if you've rented a car, chances are your car looks just like everyone else's. Now, you may think if you've lost your car in this sea of similarity, you may have to wait until your car is the only one left, but that wouldn't make for a very happy you. No need to worry. As long as you know what time you arrived at the park, the Disney employee can help you find your car. They do this because they have seen other guests before you lose their cars, realized that it creates for a very poor experience at the end of the day, and have since tracked the time they fill each row in their parking lot. Now, that's what I call creating happiness.

The service mission statement helps drive behavior when situations happen that will not be in anyone's formal job description. In order to see a change in behavior, however, it will be important to communicate the service mission statement to employees often, and position it as each employee's personal service mission statement, something everyone needs to internalize. This is an important distinction, because chances are you already have a mission statement, your employees look at it as interested bystanders and may even criticize the shortcomings when "the firm" does not achieve results. When it's your personal service mission statement, however, it is each individual's responsibility to personally deliver that experience; employees are accountable.

When there is a philosophy in place that is communicated, reinforced and demonstrated, it creates a change in how people look at and perform every day tasks. To demonstrate, I once was responsible for the stock purchase and stock option plan for one of my employers, and initially I performed my duties from a traditional perspective. I looked for ways to save the firm money and automated the process. However, as some time went on, I began to notice there were quite a few people who left the firm without ever exercising their stock options. These options had value, and in some instances the employee left thousands of dollars behind.

That is when I started to view my job differently. I asked myself why the company gave options. Options give an employee the right to buy company stock at a fixed price. If the company stock price goes up, the value of the options increases as well. Therefore, it is correct to assume corporations give stock as a retention mechanism and in order to engage its employees in the profitability of the firm. If employees leave the company without exercising their options, however, there is no value to the benefit. People don't realize what they have.

So I realized that I was not simply responsible for processing stock options efficiently. My real purpose was to improve employee morale and engage employees in the profitability of the firm, showing them the value of their holdings. I therefore made changes in my behavior. Some of the changes were large, like issuing newly created statements regularly that included the value of the options they had. Some of the changes were small. For example, I answered the phone differently. In the past, I focused on answering questions and processing requests at face value; however, afterwards, when I realized my job was to improve moral, I routinely looked at the employee's option history to see if they had exercised options before. If they had not, I asked them their goal, asked what they were trying to accomplish and explained how options worked. Sometimes people did in fact want to exercise their options, but very often they misunderstood what they had, didn't realize the tax implications, and really didn't want to do anything at that point in time. I also proactively reached out to employees who received options but had never exercised their right to sell, and whose options were coming dangerously close to their expiration date, to make sure they didn't leave money on the table.

By looking at my job differently, I started to do everything differently, and that in turn took the job and the department to an entirely new level. If you or your employees believe they don't impact the client and are just answering questions, processing paper, writing code, or exercising options, you will never be able to achieve the type of service experience you desire for your clients. Give your employees a mission or philosophy that guides their behavior, even when the situation is not defined, and give their work a higher purpose. And, before you say it's impossible to bring your job to a higher purpose because this job or that one is very simple and mundane, realize that it has been done in an amusement park and in a hotel. If it can be done there, it can be done anywhere.

Conclusion and Action:
1. Remember, service is branding your clients' experience; define what you want your clients' experience to be and deliver against that.
2. Set up a centralized service department that reports into an area of the organization that has broad responsibility across the firm.
3. Set up a dual-reporting structure for areas within the firm who have direct impact on the client, e.g. contact centers, store employees.
4. Define a service mission statement or service vision.
5. Communicate the service mission statement or vision to employees and translate it into everyday examples, so employees understand what it means to them personally, thereby giving guidelines to your employees when undefined circumstances occur.
6. Bring all employees' jobs to a higher level.

"We cannot live only for ourselves. A thousand fibers connect us with our fellow men; and along these fibers, as sympathetic threads, our actions run as causes, and they come back to us as effects."
- *Herman Melville*

Step 2: Standardizing the Experience

The next step in implementing a firm-wide service culture is establishing standards that align to your mission statement, the consistent experiences you want your clients to realize when they work with your company.

Think of the experiences you want to standardize as being similar to the consistencies franchisers set with their franchisees. If you have been to a hotel or a restaurant chain, there are certain consistent experiences you expect to have regardless of which hotel or restaurant you visit. If you went to a particular hotel chain and the experience was different or worse than the experience you expected, the value of the franchise would be diminished from your viewpoint. If inconsistency occurs frequently, the entire value of the franchise is in jeopardy.

The same approach is taken when establishing your service standards. Determine the factors that impact your clients the most, define the experience you want them to have and then deliver it. Don't leave your customers' experience to chance.

The airline industry does this exceptionally well. If you are an elite flyer, there are perks you enjoy that involve which line you stand on, your level of phone support, the order your bags are taken off the plane, and even your seat selection. This is true regardless of which airport you are in. I don't get moved to the front of the line or get to choose my seat *sometimes*; it happens consistently. Providing this defined service experience involves many different areas of the organization; together they provide an experience that makes you, as the customer, feel elite.

Service standards are your roadmap for the service you would like to provide to clients. Those standards will be determined by who you are, who your clients are, and what you are realistically willing to commit to doing. Knowing who your customers are and which customers you are targeting will help define those experiences you want to consistently provide.

TD Bank is a regional bank who understands who their clients are and has developed standards that align to their target audience. Their target market is customers who are looking for convenience; their brand promises they are the convenient bank. Their standards then reflect that commitment. Their convenience is standardized through their website, their office locations' layout, and even their branch hours. Their branches are open seven days a week, nights and all day on Saturday; talk about convenient! Their ATMs are always stocked with deposit envelopes, and every branch has Notary Publics and coin counter machines on site; both services offered for free. Around the holidays, they even offer free money envelopes, and gift cards. These standards involve many areas within the firm; and yet together they provide a cohesive service experience for the client. The standards also support their target audience and the bank's overall mission to be known as the convenient bank.

Equally important to identifying standards that align to your service mission statement, is identifying experiences that contradict your mantra and eradicating them. For example, if a firm tells you they want to be known as the premiere service hotel, and yet you are greeted by long queues on the phone, a complicated menu, unknowledgeable personnel, or a nickel-and-dime fee mentality, you would question their claim. Whenever you receive a service that conflicts with your expectations, you will unlikely use that service, visit that restaurant or hotel, or purchase that product again. Constantly evaluate the experience provided, and do away with those behaviors, processes, and products that do not support the service mission statement.

Establishing service standards will identify the areas that impact your clients the most and define what you expect that experience to be. This in turn will reduce the inconsistencies clients have with your organization that exist at many other service providers. If you doubt this, think about your personal service experiences. In many instances, whether or not those experiences were good or bad can be attributed to the service experience you had with an individual. Create standards around the experience you want your clients to have, and you reduce the inconsistencies.

In addition to the detailed service standards, develop summarized standards as well, so the summarized version can be easily communicated. And understand that you can control your clients' experience and can ensure a consistently excellent service experience, through communication, training and accountability. Your clients' experiences will be a predictor of their future business. Their experiences will drive your results.

You can apply this theory to any situation, since you yourself formulate opinions of businesses, restaurants and people based upon your experiences with them; the same is true of your clients. Their experiences will formulate opinions that determine whether or not they continue doing business with your firm. Therefore, if you want more business, provide great experiences.

Put simply: define what you want your clients' experience to be, and make that part of your standards. If, for example, you feel strongly that an employee picks up phones instead of customers being sent into voicemail or to an automated attendant, make that one of your standards. If you want employees to consistently call and confirm appointments by mailing a copy of the agenda and directions to the office before every meeting, define that as well. Summarize those standards into broad categories, such as communication, proactive service, service recovery, and training, so they can be communicated easily. In the next few chapters, we will explore, in more detail, some of these standards you may want to develop for yourself and your organization.

As we close our introduction to standardizing the experience, I'd like you to remember that even the worst of companies give good service once in a while. In fact, giving sporadically good service is what most organizations are doing; if the sun is shining, and I happen to get the right person, I will then have a good experience. But if I call at the wrong time, speak with the wrong employee, or it's raining outside, I have a poor experience. Providing good service consistently is where your department, store, or business will differentiate itself, and is what your objective should be. Defining service standards will help you achieve that.

Conclusion and Action:

7. Define detailed and summarized service standards so they can be easily communicated to and ultimately by senior management.
8. Ensure the standards are aligned to your service mission statement.
9. Identify behaviors, practices, and products that don't align, and get rid of them.

"It is one of the most beautiful compensations of life
that no man can sincerely try to help another without
helping himself."
- *Ralph Waldo Emerson*

Step 3: Connecting with Your Clients

How you as an organization connect with your clients may include company communications, such as your website, invoices, or statements; employee-driven communications, such as letters, e-mail, voicemail, or phone conversations, and what I refer to as unspoken communications, such as your store layout or employee behavior. All three types of interactions are going to impact your clients' service experience.

Clients will compare the communication experiences they have with you and your company to what they expect of you, and what they receive or perceive they can receive from other service providers. Therefore, if you tell me that your firm is a premier organization, when reviewing your company communications, I will expect your website, statements, and invoices to be state-of-the-art; I will even compare the communications from both your company and your employees to what I can receive from other companies that may not be your direct competitors, but are best-in-class in a particular category. If you tell me your firm is a low-cost provider, I will expect a no-frills service, along with low prices. I may still compare your employees with the friendly people I met at Disney, however, and I may even compare your website to Discover Cards' site, where everything is very intuitive and I have a lot of flexibility to sort, display and analyze information. Who you say you are as a firm will impact my expectations, but my perception of your firm will also be impacted by your competitors and firms who you may not even consider to be competitors.

Our second connection to clients involves employee-driven communications. This can be even more important to clients than corporate communications, because how individual employees within your organization interact with your clients will impact your clients' perception of your firm. If you don't think this to be true, consider this:

> 68% of clients leave because of an attitude of indifference from a company employee.
>
> - American Society of Quality

In other words, every single employee you hire *is* your company to your clients, and the experiences you and your employees provide can cause clients to stop doing business with you. This is why it is critical to not only focus on company communications, but also address how your employees communicate and interact with your clients. How clients are greeted or are made to feel welcome, phone conversations, and written communications all impact a clients' perception of your firm.

Very often managers just assume employees will 'just know' how to behave; we're hiring professionals after all, therefore, it is not necessary to get involved with such minutia. I remember when my son started bussing tables at a nearby restaurant. He was handed a uniform and a dishrag and told to get to work. How hard is it? You see a dirty table, and you clean it. He was showed how to clean the table, the chairs, and how to set the table, but no one told him how they expected him to interact with the clients. Thankfully, I was there and frequented the restaurant often when he first started, so I could coach him through various situations. I showed him how to greet customers, get them beverages if they requested them (instead of his first inclination, which was to tell them that wasn't his job!), and told him to not clear plates until everyone at the table was finished.

I am not suggesting that you turn your employees into robots, because there is nothing worse than a scripted employee who clearly is only going through the motions. However, guidelines and standards are imperative in order to ensure a consistent experience for your clients. How quickly should the phones be answered? What should people say when they pick up the phone? What should occur when a call is received that belongs to another department within the organization? What information should be included on employee's voicemail messages? If you don't identify your clients' experience, your employees will determine what the experience should be, and if that happens, at best, the experience will be inconsistent. At worst, you and your clients will not be happy with the experience delivered.

Now I know some of you are probably rolling your eyes at this point; we need to get involved with employees' voicemail messages? However, consider this. My son primarily earns money so he can pay for his cell phone. If you call him, chances are you'll hear his voicemail message: "Yo. This is Ben. Leave a message and I may get back to you." Now, I know you would never leave a message like this, but I have heard some pretty strange business voicemail messages; some sound as if the individual was leaving a message on their home phone or worse.

Here are sample guidelines to be considered when setting a voicemail standard, just to ensure consistency and ensure the message correctly reflects the image you'd like to portray.

- Identify your firm and the employee
- Let the caller know if you are in the office or not
- Let the caller know if you are checking-in for messages
- Give the caller alternatives in the event they need to speak to someone immediately

These guidelines are some of those you should consider when setting up your own firm's standard. If you don't set up details around your employee-communications, it is not likely that every point will be addressed by each individual.

In addition to setting up service standards around your firm communications and how your employees communicate with your clients, review those unspoken communications. Unspoken communications may characterize themselves through your office or store layout, and whether or not your office has been designed with your clients in mind.

I recently changed my grocery store after years of dissatisfaction. It is not that I hadn't tried changing stores before; I just couldn't find a store that was any better. There are many reasons I was dissatisfied, but one of my biggest pet peeves involved the store layout. No matter what time of day or night you went to this store, they were always stocking the shelves. I understand this is a task that needs to be done, but if two grocery carts were in the same aisle, you were unable to proceed because there were boxes also taking up space. The people stocking would take up much of the aisle, setting up in the middle of the aisle so as to give themselves ample room, and literally stocking in every aisle of the store. The dairy aisle, which tends to be the busiest, also seemed to be the worst. Boxes, waiting to be emptied, created a makeshift wall down the aisle, so everyone needed to shop in a single-file line. And heaven forbid you needed something on the other side of the wall. Every time I shopped there I would become frustrated by the experience; I didn't see any alternative however, since this is how most grocery stores operate. I then received a membership card to BJs; and found that the store that I now shop in designed their dairy aisles so they are able to stock milk, orange juice, and other items that sell quickly from behind. They don't inconvenience their clients. I now travel 20 minutes past my grocery store to shop, just so I don't need to deal with the obstacle course in my old store. Does the floor layout impact the satisfaction of your clients? You bet it does.

In addition to the unspoken communications that may be evidenced through your floor layout, the unspoken communications represented through your employees' behavior also impacts your client's satisfaction. If you or your employees' behavior contradicts your service mission statement, the behavior will trump the mission statement and the behavior will communicate what your firm really stands for.

"What you do speaks so loud I cannot hear what you say."
– Ralph Waldo Emerson

You and your employees can be taught to say all the right things, but be sure to review the unspoken messages, you are sending, as well. I once went into a doctors' office where the receptionist clearly had other duties besides welcoming patients. She was sending out a mailing and stacked all the envelopes in front of her, so you were unable to see her when you walked into the office. I definitely didn't have the feeling she was happy to see me. What is being communicated? "I'm busy; go away."

Another time I went into an office at a bank. At the receptionist desk were two very large plastic jars. One was filled with candy and the other was filled with money. A seemingly innocent encounter, albeit a little strange to see big jars at the receptionist desk. But, why would anyone do that? Perhaps it is the New Jersey in me and I tend to be skeptical, but let's see if you come to the same conclusion that I did. I assumed the jar of candy was for the employees and the jar of money was to pay for the candy. Why would the company put the jars at the receptionist desk instead of the kitchen, though? That's what I thought as well! They were afraid their employees would steal the snacks or the money. What is being communicated? "Our employees are thieves."

Therefore, establish standards for every manner in which you communicate with your clients, whether it be unspoken communications, corporate communications, and employee communications. Realize as well, that although you will put standards in place, the way people, teams, and/or departments will achieve those standards will be different dependent upon their situation, experience and perception. This is an important distinction, because allowing personalization of the standard creates a sense of ownership in the objective while ensuring a consistent overall experience.

To understand how this will work in practice, assume you put in a service objective that states phones need to be picked up by the third ring. How I achieve that objective will be dependent upon what technology I have available, the size of my staff, and the number of calls my department receives. The objective is the constant. How we get there will differ. Focus on establishing the objective, and let everyone determine for themselves how they will achieve that objectiveYour company communications, employee communications, and unspoken messages are all going to impact your clients' service experience. Setting guidelines and standards around the experience you want your clients to have will ensure you connect with your clients in a positive way. And consider that if you don't set standards or objectives, your employees will personally determine what they believe to be correct, information may be missing or incorrect, and your clients may hear, "Yo this is Ben …" when they call your office.

Conclusion and Action:

10. Review every communication channel with your clients, and develop standards or guidelines around those communication vehicles.
11. Set guidelines around corporate communications, e.g. statements, website, and invoices.
12. Set guidelines around employee communications, such as the greeting, voicemail message, and written communications.
13. Review unspoken communications, e.g. your store design or employee behavior to ensure a positive client experience.

"Whether we find pleasure in our work or whether we find it a bore depends entirely upon our mental attitude toward it, not upon the task itself."
- *BC Forbes*

Step 4: Owning Your Clients' Experience

I have worked with them, I'm sure you have as well: those annoying people who never follow through on anything. If you want anything from any of these individuals, it's up to you to follow up with them; they never call back, don't respond to e-mail, make commitments they don't keep, and just don't follow through in general. What's even worse, some of these people may even be nice and have good people skills, slipping like a poison into your organization. Ownership and follow-through (or the lack thereof), can make or break your relationships with both clients and employees, because everyone wants to work with people who are dependable and follows through, doing what they say they'll do.

Even something as simple as not returning phone calls or e-mails can become a nightmare to the individual waiting a response. I once went to someone's office where there were more than twenty pink message-pad messages scattered across the desk. As I was speaking with the individual (about service no less!), I felt sorry for the clients who I assumed were waiting for a call that undoubtedly wasn't likely to materialize. I've also known other people who have actually prided themselves on not responding to e-mail, feeling it showed how busy they were.

Clients want to work with employees who will be accountable for providing a good service experience. Good employees want the same thing, perhaps for different reasons. If you work with someone who doesn't follow-through, this creates extra work for the person who is conscientious. You as the conscientious employee will need to follow up multiple times, and will sometimes even do your colleagues' work yourself, in order to meet your own deadlines. If the situation exists with someone who is genuinely liked, it's even worse, because it creates morale problems for those who are expected to pick up the slack. From a clients' perspective, however, employees who don't take ownership of issues and follow through translate into bad service.

Let's look at this in practice. I recently parked at an airport parking lot. The lot was off-site, so I booked and pre-paid for it ahead of time with my credit card. Don't ask me why, but I forgot to print and bring my receipt, which it turns out, was critical when I left the lot. Now you can't tell me other people haven't done the same thing before me; and not to give excuses, but I had a lot to remember, coordinating my vacation for my family, packing, and what not. I was in a hurry when I was making my online reservation and never saw the instructions to print my confirmation and bring it with me to the airport parking lot.

At two in the morning, after a delayed flight, all I wanted to do was go home. On top of all this, after parking in the parking lot all week, I had a flat tire. The bus driver who transported me from the airport to the parking lot pointed it out to me and told me any one of the gas stations down the street would help me change the tire. Now I was really anxious to leave. I assumed the cashier would have records of my having pre-paid the parking at the cashiers' terminal, considering it would have only meant that she have access to a computer. But she didn't have any way to access my record. So I paid again. It wasn't the cashier's fault, but I definitely didn't feel she had delivered good service, either. She told me I could request a refund. Gee, thanks.

In this instance I was the owner of the issue, for if I wanted my money back, I was the one who needed to follow-up. So I did. I went to the website and attempted to print a copy of my receipt, but it seems the site didn't give you that capability after the fact. I then made copies of my credit card receipts, one charge in July and a second in the following month for the same amount. I called the company and was told to submit a copy of my receipts; consequently I faxed the credit card receipts to the number I was given. Then I waited. I should have known that they had serious issues with refunds, since one of their phone prompts was actually dedicated to refunds. A few weeks later, after seeing no credit on my account, I followed up again. Again I was told to forward copies of the receipts, again I did, and again I waited to no avail.

A few weeks later, I was scheduled to make another trip and fly again. I decided it was cheaper to park at the airport's daily lot than to pay twice. And, this is what happens to your clients when employees do not take ownership and follow through. Clients just go elsewhere, because there are lots of choices out there. Yes, they got my $75, and perhaps they have enough volume so that they can afford to rip-off their clients, serve them only once and still stay in business. Most of us don't have the luxury to try that strategy even in the short-term, however.

Let's analyze how this could have been a better experience. For one thing, even though the cashier didn't have the capability to resolve the issue on the computer (unspoken communication), she could have taken down my information, had someone look it up the following day, and credited my account. I know it was my fault that I wasn't paying close attention to the instructions on the website, but we all need to remember that our clients don't work for us and we should make things as simple and foolproof as possible. We should anticipate our clients won't do things exactly as we would like all the time.

The individual I reached out to on the phone could have also taken ownership. It is silly that this company needs to have their clients send them documentation that lets them know what happened at their own company, especially when the transaction was booked online and paid for with a credit card. What is the unspoken message when the firm is not able to pull up customer records and needs its customers to tell them what transpired? They don't know what they're doing.

If any of the employees had taken ownership, I would have had a much more positive impression. As it was, after my third attempt, I decided the $75 wasn't all that important to me and I told my friends and relatives not to use the service again either. I may also have had a better impression of their firm if any of the gas stations I went to in the middle of the night actually fixed my flat tire. After vainly visiting three gas stations all next to one another, I called AAA, who came and had my tire fixed in 15 minutes. I found out the following day, upon bringing my tire to be repaired, that there was a nail in it. Now where do you think I picked up that nail?

Simple changes in the way things are done within your business can make your clients' experience a positive one; one where employees take ownership of the experience. To look at a company whose employees do take ownership, let's look at one of my favorite restaurants, Houston's in New Jersey. I understand everyone doesn't agree; the restaurant definitely doesn't seem to cater to children, has a limited menu, and is pretty expensive. Yet I find their service is usually top-notch, and I find their wait staff clearly to have been well-trained. For example, you may ask any waiter or waitress for a glass of water, or anything else for that matter. You don't need to find the waiter or waitress you've been assigned. Everyone will pick up empty plates, or process your payment for you. The manner in which it is done is subtle, you may not even realize what is happening, but it makes for a much better experience for those who eat at the restaurant. Other clientele must see the difference as well, because I will often wait nearly two hours just to get a table. Taking ownership takes many forms, through the every day behavior of your employees.

Not taking ownership can also reveal itself in many forms. It can be demonstrated through the employee who doesn't call when they promise, gives advice for a particular issue but doesn't solve the problem, tells you to wait for your waiter or waitress so you may be helped, and the employee who doesn't meet their delivery dates.

It also may be a perception problem, however. For, there are times when you or your employees may absolutely take ownership of an issue. You are working very hard on the difficulty and doing all the right things to solve the problem. Yet your clients feel they haven't received a good service experience. How can this be?

Very often, because we as employees are so used to what is involved with a process or issue, we assume our clients know how involved those processes or issues are as well. This may not be the case however. Take opening an account at an investment firm. Many of us are not finance-oriented; even those of us who have backgrounds in accounting and corporate finance often do not consider ourselves to be investment experts. So it is with the typical investment firm client.

However these same clients have experience opening checking and savings accounts. Within five minutes they can walk into a bank, give their name, address and social security number, show their license, hand over $20 and walk out with a starter checkbook, deposit slip and access to online services. They're good to go.

So, if these same clients were to come into a financial services firm to open an account, they will expect it to take five minutes, because that is what their experience has been with a similar event they can identify with. In fact, if it is not explained to them up front that these accounts are much more sophisticated, they can do so much more with the accounts than simply move cash in and out, and there are many more laws governing them, that client will think we have not taken ownership, and are not following through with their new account opening process, when in fact we have. It is, therefore, necessary for us to set our clients' expectations; and give explanations as to what differences may exist. Without this, the client may believe no one has followed through or taken ownership on their request.

Clients make comparisons with other businesses and experiences they have all the time, making comparisons with businesses that may not even be within the same industry as yours; comparing your products and services with the experiences had at competitors and non-competitors alike. Is this fair? Not always, but we all do it. So when clients call you, expect that they may be making a comparison to the company they've called that has no menu prompts, answers the phone quickly, and has very helpful, knowledgeable employees on the other end. When they visit your store, office or branch, anticipate they may compare you with their trip to Disney World, where they remember walking into an immaculate setting and interacting with extremely friendly employees.

The point is this. Even if you don't consider a vendor to be your competitor doesn't mean your clients agree with you. They may still compare the experience you provide with the great service experience they've received somewhere else. We need to expand our world-view so that when we self-evaluate our service, we include those restaurants, corporations, banks and experiences to whom our clients inevitably compare us, and we can make much better decisions.

Conclusion and Action:

14. Make sure you and your employees are taking ownership of issues by following through on requests the first time.
15. Answer phone calls, return phone messages, and respond to e-mail in a timely manner.
16. Expand the self-critique of your service to include all firms your clients compare your service to, not only your direct competitors.
17. If you are taking ownership of issues, and yet your clients don't believe you are because they are not comparing two like services, make sure you and your employees set expectations up front and explain the difference in services.

"Many of life's failures are people who did not realize how close they were to success when they gave up."
- *Thomas Edison*

Step 5: when the Answer is "No"

Proactive service is what will really differentiate you and your firm from the competition. Putting service standards in place is necessary, but it is also expected. No one is going to rave about your service simply because you are professional, answer the phone, or take ownership. It can hurt you negatively if you don't do any of those things, but it's not as if people are going to recommend your firm to their friends and relatives simply because you pick up the phone when they call or are professional. What will really set you apart from your competition is when you look for ways to anticipate your clients' needs. Being proactive requires you to listen beyond the question asked and anticipate what your client really needs. It is what some will refer to as proactive service.

Although it may seem overwhelming at first, I have found proactive service opportunities always can be categorized into one of four groups. Every poor or great service experience will fall into one of these four categories. I realized this after surveying the clients of many different groups and interviewing the employees in the groups who had good and poor survey results to determine what differentiating factors existed between the two. I found that when certain situations occurred, the groups who surveyed well just naturally handled the situations differently. If you or your employees learn to recognize these four categories so you are familiar with the opportunity to provide an exceptional level of service, identify situations that are particular to you or your business and identify best-practice responses, you too will be well on your way to providing exceptional service to your clients.

The four categories are:

1) When the answer is "No"
2) When your clients don't know what they don't know
3) When something happens
4) When it's not your job

These four categories of situations represent types of scenarios that when surfaced, will never lead to a neutral service experience. Clients will have either a poor or an excellent service experience, when situations occur that fall into one of these categories, depending upon how they're handled.

The first category of situations that offer the opportunity to provide your clients with proactive service is when the answer is "No." When the answer is "No," your client never walks away with a neutral experience. They're either going to think that they had a great service experience or a poor one based upon how it was handled. Let me demonstrate.

I once had a person who came up to me after I spoke who told me that they would deliver great service if it weren't for the employees at the firm who gave home-office support. I always find it a little bit amusing when people tell *me* this since I'm often considered a home-office employee as well. I asked him what he meant, and he relayed a sad story. He explained to me that he had a client whose son recently passed away. When the son was still sick in the hospital, and the client was at his son's bedside, the client asked that a certain transaction be completed – a transaction that required written authorization. The employee called the home-office repeatedly to waive the need for the signature, all to no avail. The signature was necessary. Finally, the client left his son's bedside, drove four hours to the office and signed the paperwork. Horrible experience? Absolutely. But whose fault was this experience?

For when you really think about it, it was the employee who chose to stop at the "No." He kept calling his home-office colleagues to ask the same question, hoping for a different answer. Although he was told the signature was a legal requirement, he didn't pursue any other alternatives. He simply continued to ask that the need for the signature be waived. Had he accepted the answer, he could have looked for better solutions, including faxing, using an over-night service, or messengering the documentation to the client. He could have driven to the hospital himself. He could even have made arrangements with one of the offices closer to the hospital, so the client needn't make the four hour trek. Any of these alternatives would have offered the client a differentiated service experience, but the employee didn't, and stopped at the "No," thereby creating a poor service experience for his client.

Another time, I was with my son Matt at one of those video game stores. Because I am the mother of two teenage boys, you can often find me there. I am usually the person who is aimlessly hugging the wall of the store hoping their children make their selection quickly so I can go home. On this particular occasion, my son wanted a particular game and asked the employee if they had it in stock because he didn't see it. "No" was the response. No?

Now because I am who I am, and sometimes because it is just too much fun to resist pointing out the absurd, I asked the clerk if he thought that response was helpful. He seemed surprised. "But we don't have that game in stock," was his response. "I'm sure you don't. But are you getting it, if so when, can we get it from one of your other franchised stores, is it not released yet, or do you have alternate games you can recommend? Just saying no isn't really being very helpful." At this point my son is telling me he doesn't really want the game after all, and the employee is laughing, because he's realizing the absurdity of his response, as well.

However, my point with both stories is this. In both situations the answer was "No." In both situations, there were alternatives that could be offered. If alternatives were offered, a much different experience would have been had by the recipient, and the client would have been much happier.

What happens when there is no viable alternative? What if the answer really is "No"? There are those who may say the answer should never be "No," and there should always be an option. I would love to believe this to be true, but I also have come across situations when the answer was indeed "No" and there really wasn't an alternative to be had. In these cases, explaining why the answer is what it is can help a client understand that you've thought through the issue and are doing what is best for them. For example, there are businesses who must comply with IRS regulations, cannot support individual client technical requests without risking the stability of the entire desk-top enterprise, or who can't offer a particular service because it is discontinued. In these cases there may not be any alternatives. It's in these situations that you should offer an explanation, and when appropriate, offer substantiation such as a link to the IRS regulation; clients will realize you have thought this issue through thoroughly, and are not just arbitrarily saying "No" because it is easier to do so. In some cases you're even doing what is best for them. When offering explanations, please note, the reason given should never be "Because this is our policy." I was in a store the other day listening to what seemed like a sixteen-year-old manager explaining to an elderly woman that he couldn't refund her money because it was the store policy. Not only did saying this create an unfavorable experience for the customer to whom the words were directed, but everyone else in line who was listening in on the conversation, as well. Saying "It's our policy" comes across as an excuse, as if you aren't doing what is best for the client and haven't thought through your response as a firm employeeIt is easy to say that when the answer is "No" you should offer alternatives and/or explanations. However, that is only the first step. Because people get caught up in the routine, may not even recognize the opportunity, and some situations require a well thought-out response, analyze your clients' experience and create "if" "then" statements. Identify situations when the answer is "No" for your organization and identify responses that would connote best practices. Brainstorm alternatives with your colleagues and staff. Role-play the results and determine which responses would elicit the best response from your clients.

For example, if you work for a car rental agency and someone wants to rent a car at the rate offered last week, brainstorm best-practice responses as to what your response should be. Get everyone involved and increase the likelihood that your employees will consistently respond to client requests, when the answer is "No," in a best-practice manner that is going to differentiate you and your firm. Getting employees involved with the solution will make them more likely to adapt that solution.

As we've said before, everyone gives good service once in a while. Too often firms will assume that if they hire service-oriented people, their clients will automatically have a good experience. People will intuitively know what to do. However, some situations are difficult and need the benefit of brainstorming alternatives or the reason why ahead of time. Utilizing this methodology and developing "if" "then" statements will also help bring new employees up-to-speed sooner. Finally, not everyone is going to respond in a best-practice manner unless you train them to do so. Consistently give good service when the answer is "No" and you will improve your clients' satisfaction.

Conclusion and Action:

18. Each business and or department will have unique situations when the answer is "No." Identify when the answer is "No" for your business.

19. Determine how you want everyone to respond to the situations identified in step 18: when the answer is "no".

"Guard well within yourself that treasure, kindness. Know how to give without hesitation, how to lose without regret, how to acquire without meanness."

- George Sand

Step 6: When Your Clients Don't Know What They Don't Know

Often when I'm speaking with groups I'll ask who their clients are. The audience will list a litany of attributes; in nearly every case they'll agree that their clients are not experts in their business. I may go to a restaurant, but that doesn't mean that I know how to cook. I may go to a doctor, but that doesn't mean I'm a health expert. The same is true for most customers; they do business with you because they have a particular need that they themselves cannot resolve.

Even though most employees will agree their clients are not experts, they very frequently treat their clients as if they were. For example, they will use the lingo of the company with their client, as if their clients should understand the terminology. Have you ever worked with financial services firms that speak about faxing an LOA, reallocating your asset portfolio, and diversifying? It makes your head want to spin. But it's not only the financial services industry that does this. Many firms have internal or industry-specific language that doesn't mean much to the rest of us. As employees, making sure our internal or industry lingo is not used with our clients is important, since using jargon can alienate our clients. In addition, because our clients don't want to appear as if they don't understand what you're talking about, they may not ask you to clarify and may also not ask questions. This, very often, will result in the client getting something they don't want, and ultimately, a poor service experience.

As I mentioned earlier, I once managed my firm's stock option and stock purchase plan programs. In this instance, the firm's employees were my clients. Very frequently employees would call me to cash out all their stock options on the first day they were available. The stock options were available to them, so I could easily have simply complied with their request. Technically, they even used my terminology. When I asked them why they wanted to exercise their options, I often found that they simply didn't understand how options worked. When I explained the tax implications and the lost future value of their options, very often those individuals, after understanding what they had, would change their minds, and leave their options still intact. They also had increased loyalty to the firm because now they realized the value of their holdings. Clients want to appear to be knowledgeable, and may even attempt to use your language. If you don't ask questions to clarify their ultimate goal, you may inadvertently deliver a poor service experience.

In another situation, I participated on a panel for a firm's new hires, so we could welcome them to the firm and answer any questions they had as new colleagues. I was there to answer service questions, while someone else on the panel represented benefits. In this firm, as is the case with many firms, you had a choice of purchasing medical insurance for an individual, individual-plus-one, or family. So, once you had three people in your family, your premiums didn't increase, regardless of how many additional family members you had. On this particular occasion a new hire asked if she had to insure her husband, or if she could simply insure herself and her children, because "he never went to the doctor anyway." The answer given was "no, you don't need to cover your husband." Was this answer correct? Technically, yes. However, it also wasn't a good service experience. Even though this wasn't my area of expertise, I pointed out that there would be no additional cost if she did cover her husband since it seemed her children already pushed her to the maximum premium amount anyway. The new hire laughed and said "Thanks. That really was my question." Because this individual was unfamiliar with the various medical plans, she simply asked the wrong question. She didn't know what she didn't know. If you don't pick up on this and clarify your clients' ultimate goal, you may inadvertently deliver a poor service experience.

When you or your firm receive a question that seems illogical, make sure you ask yourself what the real question is. What is the underlying purpose or goal behind their question? Understanding what your clients are trying to ultimately accomplish will help you offer a much better and helpful response.

Frequently, the opportunity to offer proactive service and educate your clients will be hidden in your frequently asked questions; questions that you know many people will ask. Going back to our Houston's restaurant example, at the restaurant, they have these sugar contraptions on the table that are of great artistic design, I suppose, but don't look anything like sugar containers. Therefore, when you order coffee or anything else that requires sugar, you are likely to ask for it as the customer. However, since they know that question is frequently asked, the wait staff anticipates the question and resolves the issue before you as the customer have the chance to ask for sugar. This is how it works. If you order coffee, the wait staff will put your coffee on the table, grab the sugar container and open it for you, all with one motion. They don't even wait for you to ask. With something as simple as sugar, they've anticipated the question and educate their customers, offering a good proactive service experience.

Clients expect their service providers to be knowledgeable and available. Doing the bare minimum isn't going to make a client want to recommend your service to others, though. It is expected. When you partner with your clients, however, and understand who they are, what they're trying to accomplish and why, you are able to offer much better solutions and bring that service level to an entirely new dimension.

Conclusion and Action:

20. Identify the jargon that may not be understood by clients, and eliminate it from your vocabulary and written communications to clients.
21. Identify questions or requests received that may not make sense, or may be frequent in nature, and train employees to seize the opportunity to educate, partner, and offer advice.
22. Each business and/or department will have unique situations to provide educational opportunities. Identify educational opportunities for your business.
23. Determine how you want everyone to respond to the situations identified in step 22: when there's an opportunity to educate.

"We cannot change the past ... we cannot change the
fact that people will act a certain way. We cannot change
the inevitable. The only thing we can do is play on the
one string we have, and that is our attitude ...
I am convinced that life is 10% what happens to me and
90% how I react to it. And so it is with you ...
we are in charge of our attitudes."

- Charles Swindell

Step 7: when Something Happens

In business, as is true in all of life, things happen. Sometimes those events may be large; very frequently they are small. How we and our employees react when something happens, however, determines whether our clients have a great service experience or a poor one. This concept can best be demonstrated through examples.

If you realize you are going to miss a deadline, what do you do? Do you hope your colleague or client doesn't notice? Do you hope you are able to deliver what's been promised by the time they do notice? What if the situation is larger? What if there's an error? Do we let our clients know about the issue, or do we hope they won't notice? Perhaps it will go unnoticed and there will be no need to "fess up."

This concept is not only relevant with small events, but sometimes large occurrences. When something big happens, sometimes corporations will do the right thing. For example in 1982, when seven individuals died from Extra-Strength Tylenol Medicine Capsules that someone laced with poison, Johnson & Johnson received praise from the media based upon how they handled the situation, and has since been the subject-matter for college case studies, regarding how to successfully manage negative events. Instead of placing blame elsewhere, they recalled all their medicine, determined the cause of the incident to be a store customer, and introduced new triple-sealed packages to prevent the issue from ever happening again. While initially the market share of Tylenol plummeted, sales rebounded in a very short time period and they are today the most popular over-the-counter analgesic.

Doing the right thing, can in the long run, be beneficial for your firm. However, very often companies will try to take shortcuts when something occurs, and sometimes there are huge repercussions for ignoring the event. Recently, there was a case of salmonella poisoning that had originated at a peanut factory. According to reports, the peanut factory had repeatedly shipped product that failed the company's own initial tests for salmonella. In the most recent occurrence, when salmonella was suspected, the warning signs were once again ignored, and the company continued shipping product. However, this time, they pressed their luck once too often, and many people have been made sick by the company's decision to overlook the issue; a few have even died.

The majority of the time, ignoring the situation isn't going to result in a life or death situation, but it very well may create economic loss. I worked for CUC International earlier in my career. This firm wasn't meeting shareholders expectations; so rather than be forthright with their employees and shareholders, they decided to artificially produce the results the shareholders were expecting. Now, although I was not involved, I'm assuming this situation, as most situations that end badly do, may have started innocently enough. I speculate it may have started with a group of people believing they could make up the shortfall in the following quarter, rather than deal with the issue today. Except this time they didn't, and soon the situation snowballed. When the fraud ultimately was uncovered, $14 billion dollars of shareholder value was wiped out in a day, and many individuals' life savings and net worth evaporated.

Frequently, the events you will need to deal with won't lead to such dire straits, even if you handle the event poorly. However, there are repercussions for events and the decisions we make. What determines the outcome is what we decide to do when we initially become aware of an issue or situation. It may be an error, a client request that is not executed per the instructions, or a missed deadline.

For example, it could even be an error where you mistakenly pay someone. This issue occurred to me when a manual check was drawn in error to an employee. No harm, no foul right? Since it was a manual check, we could simply pull it. However, if the recipient reviewed her pay stub, she would realize a payment was made to her that she never received, because her year-to-date gross pay would have been increased. To make matters worse, the payment was for a service recognition award. As such, the payment would be given its own line item on the employee's pay stub. The employee could conceivably see the notation and incorrectly believe she won the award. I will have to admit, even after all this, I still did think about what the chances were that she would actually see it. After all, it would be reversed even from the-year to-date notation on the next payroll. Perhaps I could get away with it. But after a couple of seconds contemplating the situation, I decided to call, explain what happened, and apologize. And when all was said and done, I was glad I did.

First, doing the right thing, even when it isn't easy, and even when you don't get a favorable response, still makes you feel better. This is true because you now don't have to potentially lie and cover up the situation, which creates a whole new set of issues. Telling the truth also may gain the respect of your colleagues or clients, and they may feel that you are looking out for their best interest. In addition, bringing the issue to the attention of your client or partner avoids what I call the uncomfortable confrontation that occurs if you do decide to ignore the situation. To illustrate, let's assume there is an error on the account. It has been fixed, but you weren't able to fix it in time to avoid the error on the client's statement and if the client looks at it, they probably will see it. If you decide to hope for the best and ignore the error, you risk the chance that your client will see it. That may in fact generate a phone call. When this happens, they will not be pleased, and in some cases may even be angry or annoyed that the error occurred, and even more annoyed that no one realized the problem existed. On your end of this very unpleasant verbal beating, you'll be scrambling to find out why they're upset, scampering to find their original request, statement, or paperwork, and trying to remember the details. I can guarantee you won't be prepared when you receive their unexpected call.

If, on the other hand, when you realize the error, you decide to call your client, you will be prepared. You will have their statement, request, or paperwork in front of you and will have already mapped out the solution. In addition, clients or colleagues will not be upset, because it is you who called them. They didn't even realize that they had a problem. Very frequently, they will even thank you, because you are looking out for their best interest. Deal with events or issues as they come up; do not ignore them. This provides a much different experience; one in which you partner with your clients and colleagues. It also allows you to sleep better at night.

Conclusion and Action:
24. Each business and/or department will have unique every day events that occur, e.g. a missed deadline, stock outage, etc., that will provide opportunities to offer proactive service.
25. Determine how you want everyone to respond to the situations identified in step 24: when something happens.
26. Make sure employees know why it is better to proactively let clients or partners know when an issue exists.
27. When major issues occur, don't try to cover up the issue, but be forthcoming, and have a proposed solution ready.

"The person who says it cannot be done should not interrupt the person doing it."
- *Chinese Proverb*

Step 8: When It's Not Your Job

It's like fingernails on a chalkboard grating on the very fiber of your being. The words embody the very nature of an attitude of indifference: "It's not my job." Part of the reason we have more issues with this today than historically is we now tend to fragment ourselves in our firms, set up hierarchies and identify very specific roles. We have made people responsible for picking up this paper and bringing it over there. If something is in the way? Well it's not your job to move it. Sound preposterous? It happens every day.

A number of years ago, I ordered a chair and set up a delivery date for a Saturday, because I worked during the week. I was told it would be delivered sometime between 9 and 5 (very client-friendly in and of itself). I waited all day. Finally, the chair was delivered at 6pm at night. That didn't even bother me, because I really wanted that chair. There was only one problem; it was the wrong chair! I ordered this great big oversized chair, and what they sent me was the ugliest thing I had ever seen. I told the delivery person that wasn't the chair I ordered, who told me "I delivered the right chair. Look here. The tag on the chair matches the invoice. The sales person must have written up the order incorrectly. You'll have to call the sales person." So I called the sales person. "Sue, I know exactly what chair you wanted; I definitely sold you the correct chair. You'll need to call customer service." So I called customer service, and scheduled another delivery for two weeks later. Two weeks later, I again waited all day for the delivery that was scheduled for 9 – 5pm; they once again delivered at 6. And yes, they delivered the same wrong chair. When I complained about it, I heard the same responses I had two weeks earlier. The delivery person was still doing his job correctly; the sales person still insisted he sold me the correct chair, and customer service? They wanted to know if I wanted to schedule yet another delivery. To which I replied, "No, there is a reason you keep sending me the same wrong chair." And I drove to the showroom floor where I realized someone mis-tagged the chair six months earlier. Now, as just a side-note, I want you to think about how many people have the wrong chair sitting in their living room today. Did these other customers who weren't willing or able to solve this furniture company's furniture identification issues accept another chair, or give up and cancel the order altogether? How could it take six months to resolve the issue?

But my real question to you is this. Did each of those people, with whom I interacted, technically do their jobs correctly? Technically, yes they did. But I, as the customer didn't care, because I had the wrong chair.

Establishing the mission statement (Step 1), that guides behaviors when roles or responsibilities aren't defined, will help alleviate this issue from occurring. If, however, my job is simply to deliver the item that is on the invoice, issues like this will occur. On the other hand, if my job is to make sure clients get the furniture they want and to provide an excellent furniture purchasing experience, even if I'm the delivery person I behave differently when something goes wrong. Furthermore, your client shouldn't have to understand how you have structured your organization in order to resolve issues that come up. Before I had the problem with the chair, I didn't even realize there was a furniture tagging department. Honestly, I didn't want to know. In this instance, however, because the employees were so focused on their role and not their purpose, I as the customer, had to understand their organization if I were to ever have the correct chair in my living room.

Many of you work in organizations that are departmentalized and silo-d. Everyone has their very limited scope responsibility. However, if you and your employees don't realize your ultimate purpose is to provide a great service experience, and expect to step outside of your job descriptions once in a while, the client's experience will ultimately suffer.

Some of you may be saying this would never have happened at your company. The delivery person would have made the call to the sales person, who would have tracked down the issue. I, however, beg to differ, because it happens all the time. I recently heard the story of someone who bought holiday cards and in error had them sent to the address at the house she used to live. She realized she made the error within a day, but neither the vendor nor the shipping company could help her, because the cards had already been printed and shipped. The vendor had her calling the shipping company and the shipping company had her calling the vendor. She was told she would have to wait until the cards were delivered and ultimately returned, so they could be reshipped. Unfortunately, her previous residence was vacant, so there was no one there who could return the cards. Finally, after many phone calls not only to the vendor and the shipping company, but also to her prior neighbors, so they would be on the lookout for a delivery, the vendor reprinted her cards. At that point, however, she missed the opportunity to send cards in time for the holidays. Technically, it was her fault, but the issue occurred because neither the shipping company nor the vendor wanted to take ownership and help her fix the problem.

What makes this issue all that more frustrating, is most people won't actually say, "It's not my job." They will use many different variations of the phrase, however. I called someone once at their office after 5pm. I asked the person who picked up the phone for the person I was trying to contact and was told, "They're not here right now. It would be better if you call back tomorrow."

"Really," I asked in my yes-you-just-can't-let-this-moment-pass because-there-is-too-much-fun-to-be-had voice. "Who would it be better for?" For it was blatantly obvious he simply didn't want to take a message, and didn't consider it to be part of his job to do otherwise. It didn't matter that I could have been a very important client. All he knew is the call wasn't for him and it wasn't his job to take a message.

Another time, I had a package shipped to me in error. Knowing I would want my package if it were sent to someone else, I called the shipping company to let them know they delivered the package to the wrong house and should come pick it up. If it were for my neighbor, I would have delivered it myself, but they actually delivered it to the right street, wrong town. They told me, "You will have to drop it off at our shipping store." Hopefully, by this time you're realizing how much fun is really to be had out there.

"Really," I asked, "I don't think so. I don't work for you. I don't 'have to' do anything." I actually did end up dropping it off at the shipping store, because the person I was dealing with on the phone wasn't picking up on the absurdity of the situation, which made the whole situation far less fun. She couldn't understand why I thought the driver should come to my house and pick up the package that they delivered to me in error. Since I didn't want the person who was expecting a package (Who knows, it might have even been those holiday cards!) to suffer, I dropped it off while running my weekend errands a few days later.

Sometimes, the employee doesn't need to say anything. Sometimes just the behavior of your employees sends the message loud and clear. As I mentioned earlier in this book, I recently changed food stores. In addition to a poor layout of the store and employees who stocked shelves and created obstacle courses up and down every aisle, they also had very clearly defined employee roles. These very strict job descriptions created service issues. For example, if you bought too many groceries and couldn't make it out to the car, that was too bad. There was no one who worked at the store whose responsibility it was to help you, so you were on your own. If you went in for a few items and dropped one? Nope, that was not their job either. They would actually look to see what the commotion was and then turn their back on you after determining it wasn't their responsibility. I quickly learned to limit my food purchases, realizing I needed to be self-reliant. Thankfully, customers would help each other out.

I once left my cart of paid groceries to help a very pregnant woman with a small child and an overflowing cart get to her car. She obviously didn't realize the unwritten rules of the store; there was no way she was going to be able to get her overflowing groceries and her child to the car if a fellow customer didn't help out. However, I'd like you to imagine the reaction of that store's senior management if they realized this was occurring. They are clearly focused on the products, prices and the aesthetics of the store, all in an effort to get their clients to buy more and buy more frequently. If they realized their employees were undermining their objectives by avoiding customers who need help when opportunities exist, I'm sure they'd be surprised.

Sometime people don't even want to do their defined role, let alone bring their job to a higher purpose. For example, at this same food store, they frequently don't have baggers; the cashier also puts your groceries in bags. Some customers will just wait for the cashiers to finish scanning so they can bag; I always help so I can get out of there faster. I don't really mind. I do mind, however, being taken advantage of. Once, I was checking out with my manageable amount of groceries (The groceries that I would be able to navigate to my car) and bagging. I still had plenty of groceries left when the cashier finished scanning. But rather than pitch in and help me help her do *her* job, she just stood there waiting for me to finish. Are you kidding me? So I stopped bagging too and we just looked at each other for a very tense 30 seconds before she realized I would never leave unless she helped. As she slowly began to bag, I also picked up my bag again and I said, "I don't mind helping out, but realize that this is your job, not mine. I don't like being treated as if I am expected to do it."

The very sad fact of all of this is that this grocery store spent a lot of money renovating their store, increasing their services and expanding their hours, so they were open 24/7. If they had spent a fraction of that money training their employees, they would provide a much better experience, and would meet their objectives much more readily.

The "not my job" syndrome takes many forms and formats, but make no mistake about it, there is nothing that is more transparent or more annoying to your clients than employees who are more focused on their role, rather than their purpose for working at the firm.

Conclusion and Action:

28. Train yourself and/or your employees to identify every day situations that may be perceived as 'it's not my job'

29. Determine how you want everyone to respond to the situations identified in step 28: when it's not my job.

30. Ensure you and your employees know why it is better to help clients or partners even when it technically is not your job, by consistently verbalizing employees' purpose with the firm.

31. Review your service mission statement often in meetings, and use it as a guideline for how to behave when circumstances occur that are technically not anyone's responsibility.

"There's only one corner of the universe you can be certain of improving, and that's your own self."
- Aldous Huxley

Step 9: Nice Employees Who Know What They're Talking About

Service training begins before an employee ever joins your organization, because who you hire will be the single strongest factor in determining the success of your organization, and will also determine how successful your training is. If someone already feels they know everything and is not open to changing their behavior, does not care about others, or is not empathetic, no amount of training in the world will be able to circumvent that. You may have some limited success through a reward or recognition program, but you will never engage that individual's heart and get them to embrace your service vision. In addition, hiring well will impact the tenure of your employees, which will also determine whether or not your customers have a good experience. If your organization has a constant revolving door, moving employees in and out as if they are disposable, you will be hard-pressed to provide a great experience. Your employees will be barely trained, will not be motivated and most certainly will not be loyal to your organization or your clients.

This is going to seem overly simplistic, but if you want to have a service organization, hire service-oriented people. You may be able to train people on the technical aspects of a job; you will be unable to teach employees how to care about your clients. Use your recruiting process to eliminate candidates who aren't service-oriented and begin training contenders even before they become your employees. You can do this through the employee selection process; treating your potential new hires as you will expect them to treat your clients. Even if you decide not to hire someone, you will have a newly created group of people who have a favorable view of your firm. Your candidates may even become loyal customers.

Therefore, begin by treating the candidate's time valuably. Follow your firm's own service standards that have been set up for clients when working with candidates. You may do this by sending the candidate directions and parking instructions to your firm, confirming the appointment ahead of time, and making sure they have your contact information. Send paperwork ahead of time, so candidates have a chance to complete it and can arrive at your office prepared (and if they aren't prepared, you have your first red flag!). Make sure the receptionist has the candidate's name, so they may be greeted warmly, and make sure the reception-area is neat. Have the receptionist point out the rest rooms, offer a beverage, collect the completed paperwork, and have copies of the paperwork available if necessary. Begin the interview on time. Let the candidate know how long you anticipate the selection process will take, and let the candidate know not only if they have been selected, but also if they haven't been selected.

This list of standards may not be applicable for your organization; however, you can still apply the concept. Utilize your firm's service standards, whatever they are, and provide that experience for your candidates. Recognize that you are behaving this way because ultimately, if you want your employees to treat your clients well, you will need to treat your employees well, too.

If you want to hire people who are service-oriented, determine their attitude toward people. Do they like people? Are they friendly? Do they have good eye contact and poise? Do they work well in teams? Are they problem-solvers? Do they recover well from set backs? Do they follow through? Do they have good communication skills? Are they open to change? What drives their behaviors and motivates them? Rather than ask candidates these questions directly, ask for examples of their work experience and then just listen for these qualities.

Better yet, observe your candidates when they don't realize anyone is watching. Involve your administrative assistant in the hiring process and ask how the candidate treated them before you even greeted the candidate. It truly can be eye-opening. I once had a candidate who said all the right things and gave the right answers. I was impressed and ready to hire her! What I found out afterward, was the candidate was rude to my admin, barking orders before the interview. Those behaviors demonstrated the applicant's true attitude, and I didn't hire her. I knew this individual didn't really value people, and they would have treated employees and clients poorly if they weren't being watched. Their decisions would also have been based, not on what was best for the client, but what was in it for them.

Once you have hired a candidate, train them. Don't just put them in a seat and expect them to know what to do. All of your employees need to understand the history of the firm, the service mission statement and how that vision will impact their personal behavior and decision making process (regardless of what their ultimate role is). Employees should also receive technical training, so they know what to do when everything works well and what to do when there are problems. Their knowledge should go beyond their specific role, so they also understand the responsibilities of employees who hold related roles. In this way, they'll understand not only what to do, but who the work comes from and how it is used once it moves from them to the next area in the organization. Employees need to understand why certain behaviors are expected, and providing end-to-end training will help employees understand the importance of what they do, and how their role fits into the bigger picture. I once had an employee tell me they didn't impact service at all. Upon closer inspection, I discovered this person processed a key component in the overall client experience. Without this person, the entire process would have broken down! Because they had only been taught to key information into the computer, and weren't told why they were doing it, they never realized why their role was important and how they impacted the client and their colleagues.

Service training should be both structured so employees can discuss and adapt best-practices for particular situations they encounter, and also unstructured so service is discussed frequently and best-practices shared. Structured training is going to be less frequent, longer in length and more formal. It will help you communicate to employees the vision and purpose of the firm, and help employees understand how their role fits into the vision. Employees need to be able to articulate that vision to colleagues and clients. This may seem very simple, and yet people will often be hired for a job, and told to figure it out. Often they will be trained by the person who has worked there six months longer than they. The new hire begins to answer phone calls, process paperwork, or take tickets. They are as good as the person who taught them. All is fine until something unusual happens. What if your job is to open accounts? You receive a document, ensure the information is complete and pass it along. What if all the information is not complete on the document? At this point, you may reject the new account form, send it back to the client, or accept the incomplete account form and send the client a note saying that you have flagged the account and need the additional information. You may also call the client to get the information, or escalate the issue to your manager. The point is there are many different choices that may be made in similar circumstances; of these alternatives there are choices that may be better than others. If you don't train your employees and let them know what is expected, your clients will experience many different outcomes for similar circumstances, dependent upon the person with whom they work.

In addition to training employees on the history of the firm, the service vision, and technical training, it will be necessary to have a formal service training program. Anticipate getting very negative responses when you initially introduce this, however, because it seems some people feel training insults the very core of who they are. It's as if they believe that since everyone is able to recognize poor and excellent service experiences, we all must know what we're doing; there is nothing left to learn. None of *us* delivers poor service, so if the client ultimately has a poor service experience with our firm, it must be due to something, or someone else. Having asked established employees to complete service training so that best-practices are uniformly delivered, I'll hear remarks similar to these: "I know how to give good service," "I'm a professional," "I've been doing this for 25 years," "I'm insulted," "I don't need this, but my people do."

After reading through this book, you hopefully realize that good service doesn't just happen, however. It is deliberate and thought-provoking, and it's not always intuitive. There's a lot of psychology and research behind good and poor service experiences. In addition, making sure everyone is on the same page regarding your service standards is important, to ensure your clients have a consistent experience. As we've said, good service is a branding of the clients' experience and involves every single decision, conversation, technology, fee, program and product; service involves everything that impacts your client.

Formal service training is also necessary because employees need to understand the standards, and need to be taught best-practices that have been adapted into standards. Did you know, in order to take tickets at Disney, employees need to complete a two week course? The same is true for Guest Relations, although in that situation, the employees need to also pass a 4–6 hour exam. If you want to have an organization or department that is known for service, you need to formally train your employees, constantly reinforce the messages and share best-practices.

Great service organizations will be passionate about surfacing best-practice ideas and replicating them so that everyone can benefit. This can only happen through constant training and communications. Surprisingly, I've spoken with people who believe one class once a year whose focus is on service is sufficient. In addition to rigorous formal training, do you realize The Ritz-Carlton has daily mandatory meetings for 10–15 minutes? The purpose of these meetings is to focus their employees on why they are there every day. And let's face it, very often, as we go through the grind of life, we can get caught up with the function and forget our purpose. We need to constantly remind ourselves to bring our jobs to that higher level, and we can only do this through regular training and communications. Frequent communications also allow you to share and replicate the best-practices of your model service providers who simply handle situations better than others. Because there are so many different situations, exemplary service role models can learn from others as well.

Provide an environment where people can share best-practices and discuss challenges they may be experiencing. Since the purpose of service training is ultimately to inspire and change behavior, you can very effectively accomplish this through the stories that help recipients buy into your vision. If you only speak in theory, people's eyes glaze over. When you tell stories, people are much more likely to identify with the situation, remember the point, and embrace the concept as their own.

There are times when training isn't necessary, however. Sometimes all you really need to do is hold your employees accountable to the standards you've set up. I once held a training class complete with role-plays for administrative assistants. We wanted to brand the experience for callers to these employees' phones. After the class, we called the attendees to determine if their behavior changed and if they were utilizing their new skills. If we called from my desk, my name came across their phone's LCD display and they answered the phone correctly, as they had been taught. If we called from another phone, one whose owner the administrative assistants wouldn't recognize, they reverted to their old habits. It wasn't that they didn't know what they should do, they just weren't being held accountable for following through with what they had been taught. A combination of training and accountability is necessary to change behavior.

Finally, make sure your technical training also aligns with your service objectives. I once was asked to comment on technical training that came complete with role-play situations. The role-plays were designed to teach skills on specific products. However, in the documented conversations, the employee wasn't proactive, didn't educate the caller, and didn't answer the phone properly. Your service standards and service mission statement need to be integrated into all training conducted, even if it's not considered service training, in order to ensure a consistent message.

Differentiating your service experience is the result of everything and everyone within your organization being aligned and working cohesively together. Formal service training and informal conversations that surface best-practices need to occur on a regular basis in order to be successful with that goal. Your service training needs to be integrated into all other training, and all other training needs to be aligned with your service objectives. Stories that serve as examples, and can become your company's folklore, need to be embedded into the communications and training, so people understand what makes a great service experience. And it all starts with our employees.

Conclusion and Action:
32. Hire service-oriented employees; expose them to your service culture through the selection and hiring process.
33. Develop formal and informal service training at your firm.
34. Teach employees to understand the history of the company, the purpose of their job as well as the technical skills necessary so they may be helpful. Teach them what to do in unusual circumstances as well.
35. Establish constant communications with your employees, so they learn, can share best-practice responses and understand thoroughly how they too can deliver excellent service.
36. Align all training with the service teachings.
37. Hold employees accountable for demonstrating the desired behavior.

"Our lives are built one small brick at a time, ordinary day by ordinary day. With each little expression of thoughtfulness, we create something of immense significance - character, both our own and that of others."

- *McCullough*

Step 10: Ensuring a Good Experience and Recovering When It's Not

According to Webster's Dictionary, *quality control* is the system for maintaining desired standards in a product or process. Ensuring your service delivery meets your clients' expectations also requires a planned, systematic approach, which requires a review of your organization's service delivery from your client's perspective.

One way to accomplish this is to encourage your employees to use your company's products and services. It not only gives employees a broader understanding of the company's offerings, but also provides a deeper, more personal connection to the product or service that can't be appreciated through a formal training course alone. Not only should employees use the company's products and services, but they should be encouraged to surface service issues that they come across, so issues may be addressed more quickly and attended to before clients are negatively impacted.

Encourage employees to regularly utilize your firm's ancillary services, as well, such as customer service or the website. I am amazed at the number of firms who put together phone systems or prompts, websites, or other service standards and then never call themselves to realize that after four rings the caller is disconnected, the prompts don't work, the website offers alternatives that are not viable, or the voicemail is set up unprofessionally.

Do you know what the experience is for the person who calls you? Will someone pick up the phone quickly; will they answer professionally? If your clients have a poor experience, it will reflect poorly on you and your firm. Clients will also wonder if you are able to handle more important matters, since you aren't able to handle the simple issues. To demonstrate this with a recent experience of mine, I recently needed to publish this book, and as a result, I compared services and pricing from a number of different publishers. One in particular received good third-party evaluations and had pricing that was much lower than their competitors. However, their website was also riddled with spelling errors. It made me wonder if they were going to be equally careless with my work. As a result, I did not work with them. The little things matter.

Exploring this issue further, what is the experience your clients have if they shop at your store, use your products, or navigate your website? Is it intuitive; are you able to find the information or merchandise you are looking for easily? What is the experience if there is a new product or offering? How do your employees become aware of changes or offerings; are they knowledgeable? Do you know what your employees are saying to your clients? Are they friendly and professional and are they proactive, utilizing best-practice responses when speaking with your customers? For it's in the answers to these questions that you are either gathering new or turning away clients.

Technology may help you understand what your employees are saying to your clients, especially in call-center type environments, where quality-monitoring equipment exists. For all other environments, leveraging your employees by encouraging them to regularly use the products or services and to provide feedback on their experience is useful. A mystery-shopping-type solution may also be helpful.

If you are a senior manager, listen to a handful of calls on a regular basis in order to understand the types of calls and issues that are coming in, as well. Too often, managers become far too removed from what is happening, and their decisions become less effective as a result. Listening to calls will provide unfiltered information about what your clients really feel about the products and services being offered.

In addition to getting feedback from employees and senior managers, get a broad range of input from various sources, since fresh viewpoints will surface issues that you otherwise may not see. One often untapped source of valuable feedback is your new hires. New hires will see and question your products and services through unbiased eyes; in effect, they will see things as your clients see them. They will also surface issues that others, who have become used to the dysfunction in your department or organization, won't see any longer. Recognize their feedback to your organization as valuable and actively solicit their input.

A good quality program should also track errors and payments for errors, and understand and fix the underlying reason the error occurred. Determine what caused the problem and ensure mistakes don't happen again. No one expects anyone to be perfect all the time, but you had better believe a client is going to question their relationship with you if you consistently make the same mistake over and over again. One of the reasons the airlines have so few accidents, is that when something happens, they utilize this method, analyze the cause and implement technology or policy changes to ensure it won't happen again.

If you do make a mistake, apologize. It will diffuse the situation and let you move on to the solution. Too many people and firms today do not want to apologize because they don't want to admit error. They are afraid of being sued. However, nothing could be further from the truth. In a recent study with doctors, hospitals, patients, and lawyers, an apology was found to actually decrease the number of lawsuits.

Provide good service when an error is made, assure your clients it won't happen again and apologize. Providing good service may mean saying "I'm sorry" even when your client is inconvenienced, perhaps through no fault of your company. The issue in question may have even been caused by your client themselves or an event caused by nature. Saying that you're sorry it happened shows empathy, makes the client feel as if you value the relationship, and allows you to move forward and focus on the solution. For example, if you tell me your house has burned down, I can honestly feel sorry that happened to you; it doesn't mean I'm admitting fault, however. This type of empathy and apology helps build relationships with your clients. In addition, if you don't acknowledge the issue and simply try to move on, your client will continually bring up the topic until they receive the compassion they're looking for.

Please note, although there are firms who are afraid to say that they are sorry, there are other firms using the "I'm sorry" to the extreme, and in these situations, the apology is then coming off as phony, and not having the desired effect. Recognize as well, that not all people are looking for an apology. Some customers only want restitution or an assurance the issue won't happen again. Others may just love the confrontation, live to find fault with others, and like to be in charge. In this latter case your best bet is to give your customer a choice between possible solutions. Identify whether your client is the type who would appreciate an apology and a solution, a choice between solutions, or simply wants it fixed.

In general, though, when an error occurs that is the result of a mistake made by someone within your firm, apologize, fix the problem, ensure the issue won't happen again, and then recover the relationship. Consider these statistics from McKinsey and Company:

- ♦ Customers who have major problems but don't complain continue to do business with the firm at a rate of about 9%.
- ♦ Those who do complain, regardless of the outcome, continue to do business with the firm at a rate of approximately 19%.
- ♦ Customers who have their complaint resolved continue to do business with the firm at a rate of 54%.

- If you resolve the issue quickly, customers will continue to do business with your firm at a rate of 82-95%.

- Customers who complain and are satisfied are up to 8% more loyal than if they had no problem at all.

So, if we resolve our clients' issues quickly, and resolve the issue properly, we can make our clients more loyal. This can give a whole new perspective for those clients who come to you with a complaint. They are actually doing you a favor, when you realize the alternative is they simply stop doing business with you. Therefore, we should encourage our clients to bring their complaints to our attention so we can correct the issue and turn them into more loyal clients. Yet, according to the Customer Service Institute, only 4% of clients complain, the other 96% will just not do business with you again. Think about that. Here is a great opportunity to develop more loyal clients, and yet most clients just don't say anything when they have a poor experience – to you anyway. Studies show they are talking to their friends and relatives. But why would someone have a poor experience and not say anything? There are many times, I'm sure, that you have had a poor experience and have chosen to ignore the situation and decided it was easier to go somewhere else. Very frequently, clients don't surface their problems because they feel it is hopeless, the issue won't get resolved anyway, they don't want to get someone in trouble, or they don't believe it's worth their time.

And so the questions that beg to be asked here are these. What thought has been put into your firm's service recovery model? When clients complain, who do they complain to? Have the employees been properly trained in handling customer complaints? Do you, as the manager, even realize that there is an issue and if the issue has been resolved? Encourage your customers to raise issues, but make sure when they do, that the employee has been trained to listen to the client, the issues are resolved, and customers feel valued.

The perfect illustration of this point happened to a friend of mine. She was traveling and her flight was delayed, so she arrived very late, tired, and hungry. When she gave her name to the front-desk receptionist, there was no record of the reservation being made. Worse yet, there was a convention in town so there were no rooms to be had anywhere in the city. The employee at the reception desk continued to look for a room, however, and within minutes found one last room available within that hotel. My friend took the elevator up to her room, still a little annoyed that the mishap happened, and walked inside.

When she walked into the room, however, there was a fruit basket with a note apologizing for the mix-up. My friend was so pleased, not only with the fruit basket, but with the fact that they acknowledged her inconvenience. She still raves about the wonderful hotel who gave her a fruit basket; the reservation issue long forgotten.

There are a few lessons we can learn here. First, the receptionist didn't focus on who caused the error. For all they knew, my friends' administrative assistant failed to make the reservations. Why the problem occurred didn't matter at that moment, though. They had a client who needed a place to sleep. Second, the employee focused on solving the problem and did so relatively quickly.

However, this hotel also gave my friend a fruit basket with an apology for the inconvenience. On top of that, they did so late at night after most florists were closed, and were able to get the fruit basket to the room in record speed, in the amount of time it took my friend to check in and go upstairs. So how did they do this so quickly? The only way they could have possibly recovered this fast is if they had a room of gift baskets ready for such an occasion. In fact, they may have been storing fruit baskets in the room they gave her and cleared out all but one so they could accommodate their unexpected guest. The point, though, is this: This hotel had thought through their service recovery process ahead of time so when an event occurred, they were ready. Personnel were trained on the process and knew what to do.

I'd like you to note, this hotel didn't give the fruit basket before they resolved the issue. If they had, my friend would have had two problems. She would still need a room, and she would be carrying not only her luggage but also her fruit basket. No, they resolved the issue and then gave the token gift. That is ridiculous you say. Who would give a token gift without resolving the issue first? And yet, it happens all the time. When an error occurs, employees will offer a pen, t-shirt, free checking, etc. without solving the problem. I once went through a car wash before the brushless era, and received a scratch from one end of the car to the other. When I pointed out the problem to the manager, I was offered a car wash. That wasn't my problem, however. I needed someone to fix the scratch in my car. I'd then be more than happy to receive a free car wash. Teach your employees to fix the problem first, and then determine whether a token gift is necessary.

It is important to utilize token gifts sparingly, because I also know of firms who utilize this tactic too often. A friend of mine has a house full of pens, paperweights, and a host of other trinkets received from her bank each time they made an error. Many of the offenses were extremely minor, but, because there are so many gifts, they serve as a constant reminder of how many errors her bank makes.

A well thought out recovery plan is necessary in every business, and is worth the investment necessary to ensure the plan is effective. You will develop more loyal clients and be more profitable in the long run. In fact, statistics show that it is five times cheaper to keep a client than it is to get a new one. This is true because new clients typically require a lot of up-front costs including advertising, marketing, and initial paperwork that needs to be completed. New clients require more attention, because they're not used to the way business is done and frequently have more questions. Also, new clients tend to do less business with you initially, until you have proven yourself worthy of their time and effort. Conversely, clients who are pleased with their experience and have worked with you for a while are the cheapest form of advertising you could ever hope for; they'll advocate and speak positively of your services to their friends and neighbors. Therefore, work hard to keep your clients. It is much more profitable than churning through your customers. Ensuring a positive well-thought-out recovery experience is an essential part of developing that client loyalty.

Don't assume that your front-line staff, who will more than likely be the first to know about issues, will intuitively know what to do, however. Teach them how to fix issues quickly, and escalate issues when necessary. Have a well thought-out recovery process in place so that infrequent token gifts may be given after the issue is resolved.

In the event your client is one of those 96% who doesn't complain, doesn't give you a chance to recover, and stops doing business with you, develop a formal process for getting good clients back. Often clients who have worked with an organization for years will say they never even received a phone call to ask them why they left. Your lack of a response can substantiate the very reason they may have left in the first place.

Therefore, at the very least, call good clients who were profitable to your business. Find out why they left and determine if there is anything that can be done to rectify the situation. After fixing the problem, be prepared to offer a token gift, let the client know they are valued, and ensure their next few interactions with your corporation are flawless. Even if the client does not immediately want to return to your business, let them know you value them and make them feel welcome if they return. After being with your competition for a while, they may in fact decide to do that.

Put a robust multi-faceted quality program in place that includes collecting feedback, fixing the root cause of the issue, a well-placed apology, a thoughtful service recovery program, and an ex-client acquisition program. In turn, generate clients who are extremely loyal to your company and promote you to their friends and neighbors.

Conclusion and Action:

38. In addition to formal quality monitoring programs, have employees use your firm's products and services.
39. Call your phone and that of your department and/ or call center so you may experience the service delivered from their perspective.
40. Track errors and determine and eliminate the reason for the errors.
41. Have senior managers listen to calls.
42. Develop and implement a well-thought out recovery and ex-client acquisition plan.

"A goal properly set is halfway reached."
- Abraham Lincoln

Step 11: Measuring Your Progress and Listening to Feedback

In order to determine whether or not your programs are effective, it is necessary to regularly measure and/or monitor the results of the standards put in place and hold managers accountable for the outcome.

So for example, if one of your standards state that you will answer 90% of your calls within sixty seconds, measure the results. Measure those areas that are determined to be important to your clients. Monitor those items that may not be measurable but make an impression on your client, and should be standardized, such as your e-mail signatures or subject lines, adherence to company uniforms, or voicemail messages.

Hold employees accountable for producing results, but make sure objectives are achievable. This may seem obvious and yet I frequently see a firm's management put standards in place that aren't achievable and never will be. For example, one firm put in a phone service standard objective of an average of thirty seconds to answer because they wanted to deliver excellent service. Besides, that is what their competition was doing. The phone employees did their part, adhering to their schedules and percentage of time they spent on the phone. The supervisors scheduled and managed their employees, forecasted call volume, and put through the staff requisitions needed to achieve the service standard; however senior management would not approve the requisition for needed staff, making it impossible to achieve the objective. This put the entire program in jeopardy, because everyone began to question whether or not senior management was serious, not only about that particular service standard, but their service commitment in general. In fact, just to improve the statistics, employees began giving incomplete answers, artificially lowering the time it took to answer calls. Instead of improving service, the exact opposite effect was realized.

No one expects unlimited amounts of funds to be forthcoming in order to achieve service objectives, but if you put a standard in place, also ensure the resources are in place so the standard may be achieved. If not, lower the standard, or risk jeopardizing your entire service program.

In addition, be very careful what you measure, because people will work to achieve those measurements no matter what the cost, inadvertently resulting in undesirable behavior. I once worked with a firm who measured the calls handled per employee. They had a star employee; every month she broke the records for handling the most calls. Her picture was hung on the employee recognition wall. Upon closer inspection however, it became evident she handled more callers than her colleagues by disconnecting callers who had no chance of generating revenue. Not exactly a good service experience and not the intended objective when the standard was put in place.

I worked with another firm whose objectives were to lower call volume. They wanted managers to produce more client-friendly products and services that didn't result in calls; a good client-focused objective. Their solution? Riddle the phones with prompts and upfront messages, so people would be discouraged from calling.

Initially, all these measures were put in place to improve their clients' experience. None of the measurements had the desired outcome. When establishing service measurements, set them around what is important to your client, and regularly reevaluate the service measurements to ensure that they have the desired effect and you are aligned with the feedback that you receive from your clients. Focus on what is important and don't have too many measures or make it too complicated. In addition, identify lagging and leading measures to help you manage the service experience. For example, satisfaction scores are a lagging service measures. Employee turnover, especially on your front-line, is a leading indicator. You will need a combination of both in order to ensure a consistently positive service experience.

Your behavior as a leader in your department or organization is going to be more of a predictor of the success of this program than anything else though. If senior managers hold themselves and others accountable for providing a great service experience and achieving the service mission statement and standards, the employees will fall in line with the vision.

A firm whose managers walk the talk is Disney. At Disney, every single employee is expected to pick up garbage if they see it lying there. Management could simply communicate this verbally, but it wouldn't have the same effect as demonstrating the desired behavior. All Disney employees, from the person at the ticket counter to the president of the company have been conditioned to pick up any garbage that may have been left by one of their guests.

Employees listen to their senior managers, but the communication doesn't matter if the manager's behavior doesn't align. If you want your employees to treat clients professionally, you will need to treat your employees professionally. If you want your employees to treat your clients well, you had better make decisions that are in the best interest of our clients. Your employees will pick up on discrepancies between your words and behavior very quickly and what you do will always trump what you say. If service is important to you and your organization, be sure to demonstrate the actions you want to see in your employees, especially when you think no one is watching.

Listening to feedback from your clients is also important. You may want to do formal surveys, for example. My only caution with this approach is that when you are designing your surveys, ensure they are actionable, let clients know what you've done with their feedback after they've completed the survey, and don't let client feedback impact compensation directly. If you do impact employee compensation, you risk employees who are incented to scam the system, either by pre-selecting who the survey is mailed to, or even worse, asking clients to give them certain responses. As I mentioned earlier, I have purchased two cars from the same car dealer, nine years apart. I really like the car. I've also mentioned that I avoid the service department whenever possible. However, every time I have been there for service, they have asked me to give them "excellent" ratings on the survey that inevitably arrives in the mail. I have even been told on more than one occasion that it impacts their compensation, so I feel guilty for responding anything but "excellent." I finally asked them to stop surveying me; since it is obvious their goal is not to improve my experience, but theirs and they are scamming the system to get a particular score in an effort to make more money.

More often, there is great hoopla about initiating a new survey, but once it is complete, there is no action taken. Some surveys can be quite involved, too! Can you imagine being asked for your opinion, taking the time to complete the survey, giving very specific feedback, and then see nothing change? Your perception of that firm will not remain as it was before the survey was sent, if this is your experience. It is very important to ask for feedback, and then let your clients know what you've changed as a result. Phrases such as "Because of your feedback ..." when addressing future mailings to clients can be one very effective way of letting your clients know you listen.

Sometimes you can find out what your clients think even without asking them, however. Just conduct regular Google searches. You may be surprised at what people will post online and will find out the sentiment and the experiences of your clients in a timelier manner as well. You may also discover things about your company that wouldn't be surfaced in surveys or focus groups.

Other simple methods of getting feedback shouldn't be overlooked either. One such methodology that may work is implementing a suggestion box. If you do utilize this method, however, let your clients know that you value their feedback, read the responses on a regular basis and let them know what changes you have made based upon their feedback. Too often, putting a suggestion into the suggestion box seems like dropping off an idea into the abyss, never to be heard from again. But it needn't be that way. One company who has very effectively implemented a suggestion box strategy is Stew Leonards, with multiple stores in Connecticut. This store is listed in the Guinness Book of World Records as the highest grossing store per square foot in the world. To shop at Stew Leonards is an adventure, as you'll frequently see employees dressed as barnyard animals, handing out free samples. Their suggestion box receives more than 100 comments every day, and customers will even show up on the weekend in order to participate in monthly management meetings. Can you imagine your clients so interested in your success, that they're willing to give you time on the weekend?

Let clients know you value their opinion and will do something with their feedback. Your clients will be happy to share and partner with you in order to improve the service experience.

Conclusion and Action:

43. Put measurements in place that track the progress of your firm, department, store or branch against your service standards.
44. Periodically monitor those standards that can't be easily measured.
45. Hold yourself and your employees accountable for results. If standards are unachievable, lower the standard.
46. Align your behavior with your stated objectives.
47. Get feedback, utilizing various sources: surveys, employees, new hires, the internet, and even suggestion boxes.
48. Take feedback seriously and let your clients know what you changed as a result of their feedback.

"Too often we underestimate the power of a touch, a smile, a kind word, a listening ear, an honest compliment, or the smallest act of caring, all of which have the potential to turn a life around."

-Leo Buscaglia

Step 12: Using Recognition Programs to Foster Your Service Culture

Because creating a service culture requires a change in behavior, positive recognition is a critical component to reward and encourage the behavior you want replicated. Formal and informal rewards should be generated, so that recognition can be spontaneous and immediate, while other recognition is more well-thought out and ceremonial. In every instance, recognition should be given to employees for something very specific that can be tied back to the firm's service standards.

I've implemented service recognition programs in the past, and often receive nominations that read something like this:

> "Sally is so great, it's impossible to pick one reason why she should win the award."

Well, if Sally is so great, you should be able to identify something she does; if you can't, Sally won't win.

I've also known departments or companies who have set up a recognition program where ultimately everyone wins. "Jareth is the employee of the month, because it's his turn." In order to be effective, breathing cannot be the prerequisite to earning a service recognition award; it diminishes the importance of the award, and instead of motivating employees to deliver better service, it has the opposite effect. Build your recognition programs around specific desired employee behavior and create a library of great service stories that become part of your firm's folklore. Give employees concrete examples as to what is recognized and rewarded to help them understand what good service looks and feels like, and help employees understand what they need to do to also receive recognition.

Although the reasons people win should be specific, the stories should also be realistic and reflect best-practices that can be replicated. The winners should also be in good standing within the firm. You don't want to give someone an award one week and then fire them the next. It just doesn't send a good message. Choose winners who are good overall role-models who did something specific that others can replicate. Recognize the award winners at a company event. Use a variety of methods to recognize your winners. Take pictures, write the story for the company newsletter, speak during the meeting about what was done, and give the recipient money, a plaque, or letter. Make the award special and one that not too many people receive so the awards given are meaningful. If the award is given correctly, it can have a tremendously positive impact on morale, since recognition frequently goes to those hardworking front-line individuals who are often overlooked by an organization, but truly care about your clients.

In addition to the rare large-scale awards, give small and frequent appreciation for positive behavior. This recognition may be more informal and can include distribution of token gifts, gift cards, balloons, a luncheon, or thank you notes. Your recognition does not need to cost a lot of money, but it should be visible and draw the attention of the recipient's colleagues, so people talk about what was done to earn the award. And don't overlook the personalized thank you note. When genuine, a thank you note may mean more than you realize. I will often see thank you cards posted in employees' cubicles long after the message was sent.

You may also devote bulletin boards to client letters, and make recognition part of your staff meetings. This will help remind everyone why they are working, will serve as a reinforcement mechanism when you tie the recognition back to the mission statement and standards, and provide a vehicle for sharing best-practices.

If the idea for why the employee is receiving recognition is really good, and impacts your clients frequently, convert the best-practice idea into a standard that everyone replicates; continuously tying behavior back to the service mission you are trying to achieve.

Creating a culture where service is recognized and rewarded will encourage more of the same behavior in your employees. Creating a culture of recognition will create an environment where best-practices are shared and adapted and employees are valued. It also makes work much more fun. Focus on an employee's positive behavior and you will get more of the same.

Conclusion and Action:

49. Put in place a major service award, and many recognition programs; utilize bulletin boards and staff meetings to showcase award recipients and discuss best-practices.

50. Turn the best of your best-practices into service standards.

"Much of the good that might have been achieved in the world is lost through hesitation, faltering, wavering, vacillating or just not sticking with it."

- William Bennet

Conclusion: Beginning your Journey

Whenever I have workshops, I always ask participants to share their personal service stories. At one such workshop, I had a volunteer who raised her hand excitedly, anxious to share. She told the story of an experience she had fifteen years earlier. I told her it must be memorable if she remembered what happened fifteen years earlier, and she assured me that it was. In this particular instance, she wanted to purchase a particular item, and kept going back to the same store to buy it. Six times she went to the store; six times the store was out of stock. Finally the sixth time, an employee told her he'd write down her name, and call her when the item came in. He did; he actually called her! She was so happy, she wrote the president of the company a letter, letting him know what a valuable employee he had. She hoped the employee won an award. At the end of her story, my eager volunteer looked at me smiling, remembering her experience. I clearly didn't respond as she expected, although my response probably reflects what you're probably thinking right now as well.

"That is the saddest story I've ever heard", I said.

"No", she insisted, "it was a great service experience!"

I asked her what she thought the experience was for subsequent customers to the store who similarly wanted to purchase an item out of stock. She reflected for a moment, and then stated the obvious. Subsequent customers probably had the same experience she had the first five times.

So is the situation at most businesses today. The problem isn't that there aren't good service experiences to be had. The problem is that the good experiences aren't consistent because the opportunity to recognize best-practices and to replicate them has been missed; the organization is not aligned. If you don't systematically identify and replicate best-practices and provide a consistently good service experience, you will be similar to the organization in this story, which has one customer advocating their business every fifteen years, instead of literally thousands of customers telling their friends and neighbors they should do business with them, because you constantly and methodically provide positive experiences. As we've said before, everyone gives good service sporadically, even the worst firm out there. That is not where you are going to differentiate your firm from your competition; it is not where you want to be.

This example does bring up the issue as to why everyone doesn't offer great service, however, and I have found there are a number of mistakes that frequently prevent companies from being good service providers. You can now avoid these mistakes, just because you now understand what's involved with offering a great service experience. Let's summarize them, and which steps in our book addressed these issues.

Mistake #1: Believing service will happen without a concerted effort is one major mistake most people make (Steps 1, 2, 3, and 4). After having read this book you no doubt realize great service only occurs after a conscious, rigorous undertaking that involves everyone within the organization. The good news is you have the ability to impact your customers' experience when you define the experience you want your clients to have. If you leave your customers' interactions to chance and don't define the experience you would like them to have, your customers will have erratic service experiences based upon the employee they work with and the situation. Achieving the objectives is hard work, and involves training (Step 9), hiring (Step 9), rewards (Step 12), and measurements (Step 11).

Mistake #2: Not hiring service-oriented people (Step 9) and aligning the entire organization (Step 1) is a second error I frequently see. Who you hire is probably the single most important decision you make that will determine whether or not you achieve your service objective. Who you hire is not only important when employing your front-line employees, but when everyone is hired into the organization. Everyone in the organization impacts your customers experience directly or indirectly. Aligning the organization, so that everyone is held accountable for providing a good client experience is imperative, and setting up the right organizational structure is necessary. If the organization is not structured nor aligned to achieve your service objectives, senior managers may implement solutions that meet their short term goals, but those solutions may not be in the best interest of the client. I once consulted at a company that kept developing new programs, products and services that clearly were not client-friendly. As we were cleaning up what had been already created, new issues were being developed daily. Unless everyone is aligned, you and your clients will continue to experience similar situations.

Mistake #3: Limiting the scope of service to one area, such as measurements (Step 11), training (Step 9), recovery (Step 10), or proactive service (Steps 5, 6, 7, and 8), and expecting that focus to resolve all service issues is the third major issue I frequently come across. Changing the culture needs a vision or mission statement to be established (Step 1), expectations communicated and a multi-faceted approach to achieve that vision. By addressing service on different levels, you will ensure everything is reviewed from the client's perspective, and address the diversity of motivating factors for different employees. By limiting your scope, you may also limit your impact which may in turn result in lost interest. It is acceptable to pinpoint your focus for a period of time, but understand if you only address how people answer the phones, and yet the underlying processes or products still have major service issues, your results will be mediocre at best and people will soon become disenchanted. Likewise, if you focus on the products, so that your products are all top-of-the-line and client-friendly, but don't spend time on who you hire, or how you train your employees, you will similarly have only mediocre results. Changing the culture requires you to identify the strategy, involve people throughout your organization or department, prioritize what will happen when, and often revisit how you will achieve your strategy.

Mistake #4: Finally, the biggest error I see companies make, that will surely sabotage your service aspirations, is forgetting that service is a never-ending long-term journey. This is a two-fold issue. First, there will always be short-term issues that will divert the attention of senior managers when prioritizing resources and focusing the attentions of the organization. Second, people may become disenchanted the longer they wait for results, and not realize the incremental impact that is being made over time.

Let's deal with the multiple priorities issues first, because this will exist in all types of economic climates. If the environment is favorable, the temptation will be to focus on short-term sales and growth; the opportunity cost with missed revenue will be overlooked. Conversely, if the environment is unfavorable, there will be many emergencies that need to be addressed. Adding to the problem of dealing with multiple priorities is the very nature of service. For, if we give our client a good service experience today, ultimately it will impact our long term results, sales and profitability; however, it may take years for us to realize the impact. Unfortunately, if we give poor service today, it may take a while for us to realize that impact; and therefore it may not seem like a pressing matter that needs to be addressed immediately. The temptation is to focus on other priorities and let service slide. Similar to the issue that becomes evident in the story where my workshop attendee received great service because they happened to speak to the right person at the right time, service needs to be a consistent priority in all economic environments and all situations in order to be considered a true differentiator.

The second issue, that of employees becoming disenchanted because service doesn't provide immediate results can be addressed by setting your employees' expectations upfront. Let me give you two examples. Let's say your employee delivers a great service experience to a client. The client walks away very happy. The employee doesn't necessarily know if that experience has made a difference, however, and may in fact never know. Indeed, it might take a long time before the client is reminded of the good experience. At that point the client may or may not tell someone else. If your employees expect a one for one return on their service investment made with clients, they will soon become disheartened, and will be less likely to deliver a good service experience in the future. Similarly, and on a larger-impact level, let's say you want to differentiate the service you provide but realize you have many employees who aren't service-oriented. This one issue alone will take a long time to correct. Set expectations initially, so employees realize this is a journey you are embarking upon, and clearly communicate your service vision and expectations. Understand as well that changing the culture will take time, there will be naysayers, and you may be detoured along the way. In addition, decisions cannot be made in a vacuum of the environment, and alternate paths or different standards may be put in place as the environment changes that bring you to your destination. Understanding and communicating up front that this journey will take time and there will be adjustments made as new information surfaces is essential so people do not become discouraged and give up when roadblocks surface.

Develop a service mission statement or vision (Step 1) so everyone understands their purpose within your organization. Cohesively align everyone in your firm to build a comprehensive strategy through the products and service offered and quality (Step 10), training (Step 9), communications (Step 3), measurements (Step 11), and rewards (Step 12) designed to achieve the desired outcome. Anticipate that there will be those who won't buy into the concept, those who may feel the service experience involves everyone but them, and those who may have historically been successful despite the fact they have delivered poor service, who will resist change.

Implementing a successful service strategy is not going to be an easy journey; if it were, everyone would be doing it. Furthermore, you will never reach your destination, since environmental factors, competitive factors, and internal factors are constantly changing. Defining what you want your clients to experience and delivering against that objective most of the time is possible, however. Being on the right track means your employees, shareholders, and clients become advocates of your firm. At that point the journey becomes worth it.

Final Thoughts

As I complete this book, the economy is facing unprecedented challenges; many are comparing it to the Great Depression. People are losing their homes, their jobs, and their security. Given my history, and the fact that this is the fifth time I've been through change of this nature, I'm even beginning to believe this may be personally my fault. Okay, perhaps not, but I wouldn't be truthful if I didn't also say that I can't believe I'm going through this again.

I'm also grateful. For, similar to how my circumstances historically provided the catalyst that motivated me to finally complete my second bachelors degree, certifications, and my MBA, this economy has also been the criterion that spurred me to finally write this book. I appreciate that my circumstances have provided an insight I may not have otherwise developed, and a motivation to accomplish much more than I would have achieved if life had been too easy. I also realize that I have much to be thankful for. I have great faith, great family, great friends, and good health. Many others are not so fortunate. Perhaps you too, have had difficult circumstances you have needed to overcome, and feel discouraged that here is yet another obstacle in your path. I challenge you to look for the doors and opportunities that may be opening, just as other doors and opportunities may be closing, and use these circumstances as the catalyst to make the change you've been contemplating for a while.

As you've read through this book, you may also be thinking this is the wrong time to implement a service strategy; in this environment you're simply trying to survive. You may feel there are more important fires that demand your attention and cannot be ignored. To these arguments, there are a few thoughts that come to mind.

Primarily, many of the ideas I've given you can be implemented with little or no money, by reallocating resources that already exist, or by establishing teams within the organization to plan, implement and maintain tactics developed. In addition, even those items that require some money can be accomplished economically, with a little creativity.

For example, I have been known to utilize online training courses instead of a much more expensive classroom-led alternative in order to ensure a consistent message across the enterprise, with follow-up manager led meetings, so the concepts can be discussed, practiced and adapted for individual circumstances. The cost is minimal but the impact considerable.

I have also used creative and already established means to communicate and reiterate the importance of service, including three-minute videos to spoof current behavior, employee service fairs, staff meetings, existing newsletters and other employee communications.

Even something as seemingly complicated as reorganizing the firm into a matrixed organization can be implemented cost effectively, when you realize that resources are simply being reallocated. In fact, in many instances, by deploying this tactic you will actually need fewer resources, because it results in employee resources being centrally managed, instead of independently administered. The point is this, with our 12 step strategy and 50 tactics, if you implement the tactics thoughtfully and creatively, you can achieve maximum impact for a minimal investment.

Secondly, I've found there never is a 'right' environment. When things are going well, management wants to focus on sales and growing the business. When the environment is poor, they focus on cost savings. There is an advantage to implementing a service strategy during weaker economic times, however, because when business is thriving, it's hard to compete with the many more exciting things going on. In good times, in addition to sales and growing the business, managers may be busy building new technology, adding new products, hiring, and making acquisitions. Some of those decisions may be made with the best interest of the client in mind; many of those decisions may be made without. Therefore, if you implement a service strategy during peak economic times, you will need to compete with other initiatives, and not only will you have to address the decisions made already, but all of the change inevitably in progress. If on the other hand, you implement a service strategy during weaker economic times, there are fewer initiatives that you will need to compete with: less technology, fewer new products, and fewer new hires. It may actually be an easier climate to change the culture, because employees also have more of an incentive to change their behavior in order to ensure job security.

Finally, there is a lot of competition out there; consumers are becoming much more discerning when deciding when and if to spend their money and they are less tolerant with poor service than they ever have been. By implementing a comprehensive service strategy, one in which you bring employee's jobs to a higher level, you define the experience you want your clients to have; thereby putting yourself in control of your clients' experiences. Ultimately you achieve a competitive advantage, and turn your clients and your employees into advocates, creating some of the cheapest advertising around. By ensuring your clients' experience is consistently excellent, you will ultimately have a better chance at weathering this storm.

In much the same way your personal journey will inevitably be riddled with detours, bumps and roadblocks, your service journey will be the same. If you anticipate that along with success, you will also realize these inevitable setbacks and failures; you will help lessen your disappointment and your initial inclination to give up when this occurs. Furthermore, if you learn to use the setbacks as catalysts, you can use the experience to initiate positive change. Ultimately your success will not be dependent upon your circumstances, but your attitude, maturity and insight gained through perseverance.

Summary of the 12 Steps and 50 Tactics

Step 1: Beginning the Journey
1. Remember, service is branding your clients' experience; define what you want your clients' experience to be and deliver against that.
2. Set up a centralized service department that reports into an area of the organization that has broad responsibility across the firm.
3. Set up a dual-reporting structure for areas within the firm who have direct impact on the client, e.g. contact centers, store employees.
4. Define a service mission statement or service vision.
5. Communicate the service mission statement or vision to employees and translate it into everyday examples, so employees understand what it means to them personally, thereby giving guidelines to your employees when undefined circumstances occur.
6. Bring all employees' jobs to a higher level.

Step 2: Standardizing the Experience
7. Define detailed and summarized service standards so they can be easily communicated to and ultimately by senior management.
8. Ensure the standards are aligned to your service mission statement.
9. Identify behaviors, practices, and products that don't align, and get rid of them.

Step 3: Connecting with Your Clients
10. Review every communication channel with your clients, and develop standards or guidelines around those communication vehicles.
11. Set guidelines around corporate communications, e.g. statements, website, and invoices.
12. Set guidelines around employee communications, such as the greeting, voicemail message, and written communications.
13. Review unspoken communications, e.g. your store design or employee behavior to ensure a positive client experience.

Step 4: Owning Your Clients' Experience
14. Make sure you and your employees are taking ownership of issues by following through on requests the first time.
15. Answer phone calls, return phone messages, and respond to e-mail in a timely manner.
16. Expand the self-critique of your service to include all firms your clients compare your service to, not only your direct competitors.

17. If you are taking ownership of issues, and yet your clients don't believe you are because they are not comparing two like services, make sure you and your employees set expectations up front and explain the difference in services.

Step 5: When the Answer is "No"
18. Each business and or department will have unique situations when the answer is "No." Identify when the answer is "No" for your business.
19. Determine how you want everyone to respond to the situations identified in step 18: when the answer is "no".

Step 6: When Your Clients Don't Know What They Don't Know
20. Identify the jargon that may not be understood by clients, and eliminate it from your vocabulary and written communications to clients.
21. Identify questions or requests received that may not make sense, or may be frequent in nature, and train employees to seize the opportunity to educate, partner, and offer advice.
22. Each business and/or department will have unique situations to provide educational opportunities. Identify educational opportunities for your business.
23. Determine how you want everyone to respond to the situations identified in step 22: when there's an opportunity to educate.

Step 7: When Something Happens

24. Each business and/or department will have unique every day events that occur, e.g. a missed deadline, stock outage, etc., that will provide an opportunities to offer proactive service.

25. Determine how you want everyone to respond to the situations identified in step 24: when something happens.

26. Make sure employees know why it is better to proactively let clients or partners know when an issue exists.

27. When major issues occur, don't try to cover up the issue, but be forthcoming, and have a proposed solution ready.

Step 8: When It's Not Your Job

28. Train yourself and/or your employees to identify every day situations that may be perceived as 'it's not my job'

29. Determine how you want everyone to respond to the situations identified in step 28: when it's not my job.

30. Ensure you and your employees know why it is better to help clients or partners even when it technically is not your job, by consistently verbalizing employees' purpose with the firm.

31. Review your service mission statement often in meetings, and use it as a guideline for how to behave when circumstances occur that are technically not anyone's responsibility.

Step 9: Nice Employees Who Know What They're Talking About

32. Hire service-oriented employees; expose them to your service culture through the selection and hiring process.
33. Develop formal and informal service training at your firm.
34. Teach employees to understand the history of the company, the purpose of their job as well as the technical skills necessary so they may be helpful. Teach them what to do in unusual circumstances as well.
35. Establish constant communications with your employees, so they learn, can share best-practice responses and understand thoroughly how they too can deliver excellent service.
36. Align all training with the service teachings.
37. Hold employees accountable for demonstrating the desired behavior.

Step 10: Ensuring a Good Experience and Recovering When It's Not

38. In addition to formal quality monitoring programs, have employees use your firm's products and services.
39. Call your phone and that of your department and/ or call center so you may experience the service delivered from their perspective.
40. Track errors and determine and eliminate the reason for the errors.
41. Have senior managers listen to calls.

42. Develop and implement a well-thought out recovery and ex-client acquisition plan.

Step 11: Measuring Your Progress and Listening to Feedback

43. Put measurements in place that track the progress of your firm, department, store or branch against your service standards.
44. Periodically monitor those standards that can't be easily measured.
45. Hold yourself and your employees accountable for results. If standards are unachievable, lower the standard.
46. Align your behavior with your stated objectives.
47. Get feedback, utilizing various sources: surveys, employees, new hires, the internet, and even suggestion boxes.
48. Take feedback seriously and let your clients know what you changed as a result of their feedback.

Step 12: Using Recognition Programs to Foster Your Service Culture

49. Put in place a major service award, and many recognition programs; utilize bulletin boards and staff meetings to showcase award recipients and discuss best-practices.
50. Turn the best of your best-practices into service standards.

Contact Information

I'd love to hear from you! Send me your service stories, questions, challenges or feedback to my newly constructed website TheServiceJourney.com. I'll get back to you within 48 hours. You'll also find additional resources, tips, or answers to some frequently asked questions there as well.

Additional copies of this book may be ordered on amazon.com or barnesandnoble.com. To order more than 50 copies and receive a quantity discount, go to my website at TheServiceJourney.com, I'd be happy to work with you and your organization.

Notes

Forward

Norris, Floyd and Henriques, Diana B. "3 Admit Guilt In Falsifying CUC's Books". *The New York Times.* 6/15/2000.

Step 1

Reicheld, Frederick F., *The Loyalty Effect.* Boston, Massachusetts: Harvard Business School Press, 1996. 20.

Jeff Kober. mouseplanet.com. *I've Lost My Car.* 1/10/2008

Neufeldt, Victoria; Guralnik, David B. Third College Edition Webster's New World Dictionary of American English. Cleveland and New York: Simon and Schuster, Inc. 1988. *service*

Step 7

Lewin, Tamara. "Tylenol Posts an Apparent Recovery". *The New York Times.* 12/25/1982.

from news services. "Peanut company files bankruptcy." *The Chicago Tribune.* 2/14/2009.

Norris, Floyd and Henriques, Diana B. "3 Admit Guilt In Falsifying CUC's Books". *The New York Times.* 6/15/2000.

Step 9

The Ritz-Carlton Hotel Company, LLC. *Legendary Service at the Ritz-Carlton.* 2006. 16.

Connellan, Tom. *Inside the Magic Kingdom.* Austin, Texas: Bard Press, 1996. 141.

Step 10

Neufeldt, Victoria; Guralnik, David B. Third College Edition Webster's New World Dictionary of American English. Cleveland and New York: Simon and Schuster, Inc. 1988. *quality control.*

Schmidt, Debra. "A Simple Apology Can Spare You a Lawsuit." Unarchived Articles. 8/2/2007.

Levering, Robert and Moskowitz, Milton. "100 Best Companies to Work for 2008." *Fortune.* 1/22/2008.

Levering, Robert and Moskowitz, Milton. "Top 50 Employers." *Fortune.* 1/22/2008.

fundinguniverse.com. *International Directory of Company Histories*, Vol. 56. St. James Press, 2004.

US. Office of Consumer Affairs: It's five times cheaper to keep a client than to get a new one.

House, Dawn. "Try Customizing your Approach to Customer Service." *The Bergen Record.* 12/05/2007.

Griffin, Jill. *Customer Loyalty.* San Francisco, California: Jossey-Bass, 2002.

Step 11

Kober, Jeff. *mouseplanet.com.* "At Disney, Everyone Picks Up Trash!" Thursday, August 30, 2007.

References and Recommended Reading

Connellan, Tom. *Inside the Magic Kingdom.* Austin, Texas: Bard Press, 1996.

Griffin, Jill. *Customer Loyalty.* San Francisco, California: Jossey-Bass, 2002.

McCullough, Donald. *Say Please, Say Thank You.* New York: G.P. Putnam's Sons, 1998.

Reicheld, Frederick F., *The Loyalty Effect.* Boston, Massachusetts: Harvard Business School Press, 1996.

Reicheld, Frederick F., *Loyalty Rules.* Boston, Massachusetts: Harvard Business School Press, 2001.

Reicheld, Frederick F., The Ultimate Question. Boston, Massachusetts: Harvard Business School Press, 2006.

Snow, Dennis, *Lessons from the Mouse.* Sanford, Florida: DC Press, 2009.

Zemke, Ron, *Delivering Knock Your Socks Off Service.* New York: AMACOM, 2003.

Lightning Source UK Ltd.
Milton Keynes UK
18 August 2009

142789UK00001B/42/P